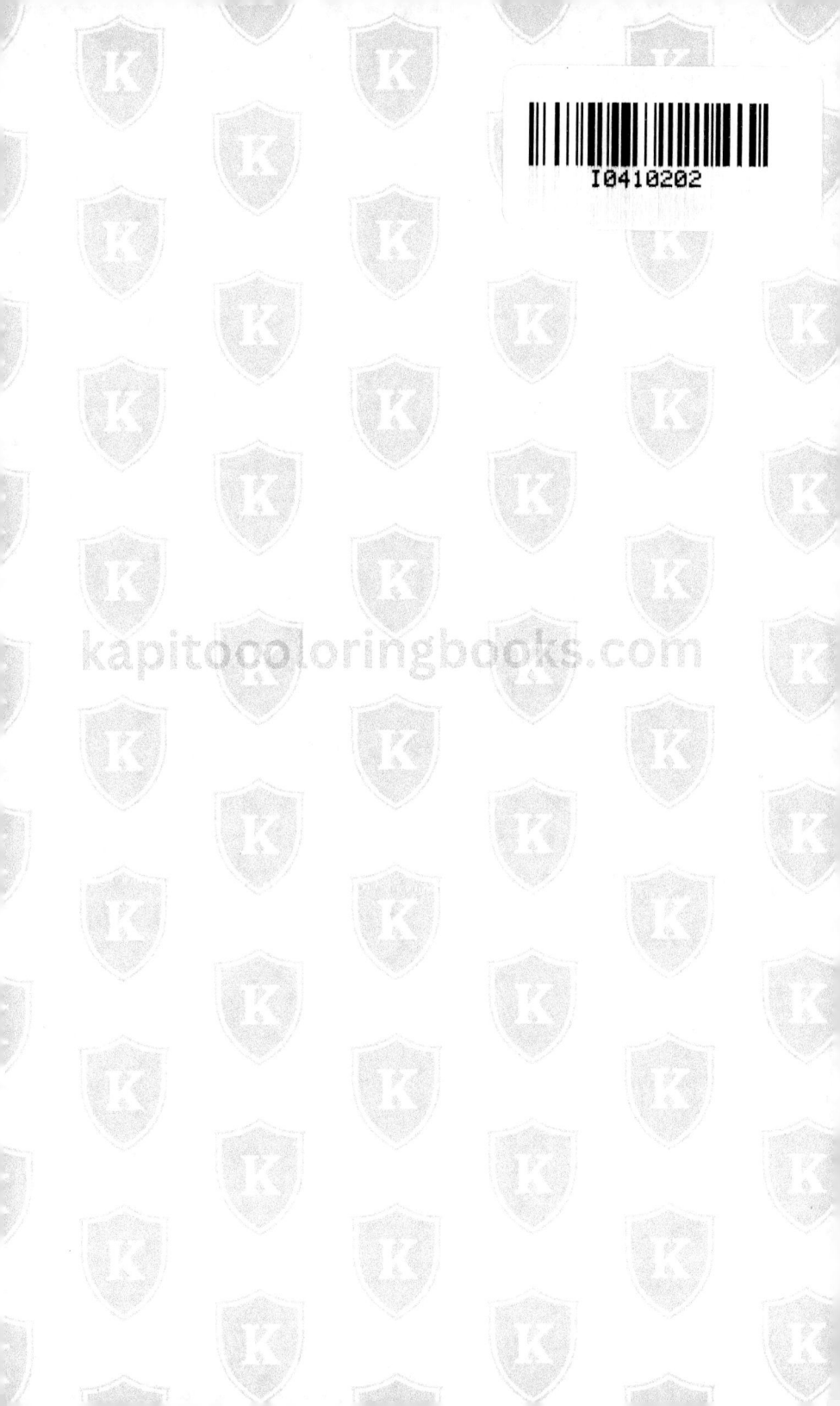

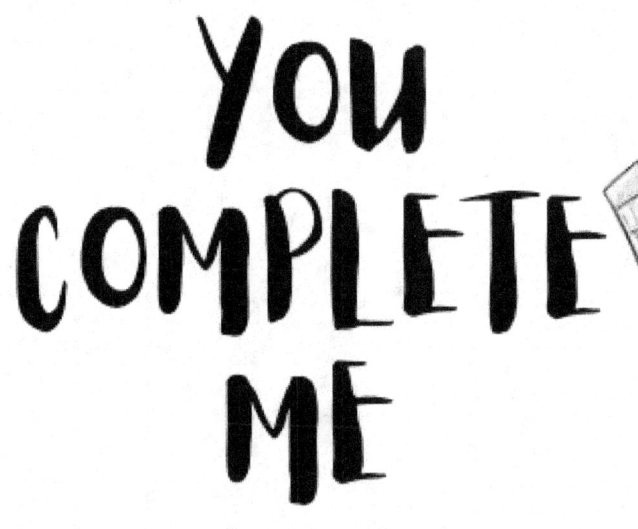

YOU COMPLETE ME

Fun & Easy Prompts to Help Defeat Artistic Block

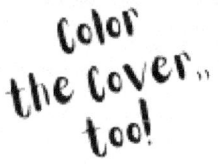

Color the Cover, too!

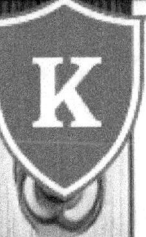

A Kapito Art Book

"I have a block, it's big and black.
It sits upon my stiff, straight back.
It ate my mind, it disappeared,
now it's gone, vanished, cleared..."

-Kapito

YOU COMPLETE ME

Fun & Easy Prompts to Help Defeat Artistic Block

www.kapitocoloringbooks.com

Here's a little teacup, short and stout. Using whatever medium you'd like, color it in. You decide the colors.

Finished? Now draw someone holding the cup and enjoying the tea. Color that in as well...

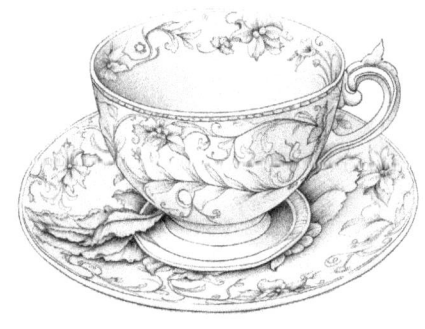

Think about the person you drew. Close your eyes and imagine them going about their day. Focus on the sights, smells, and sounds.

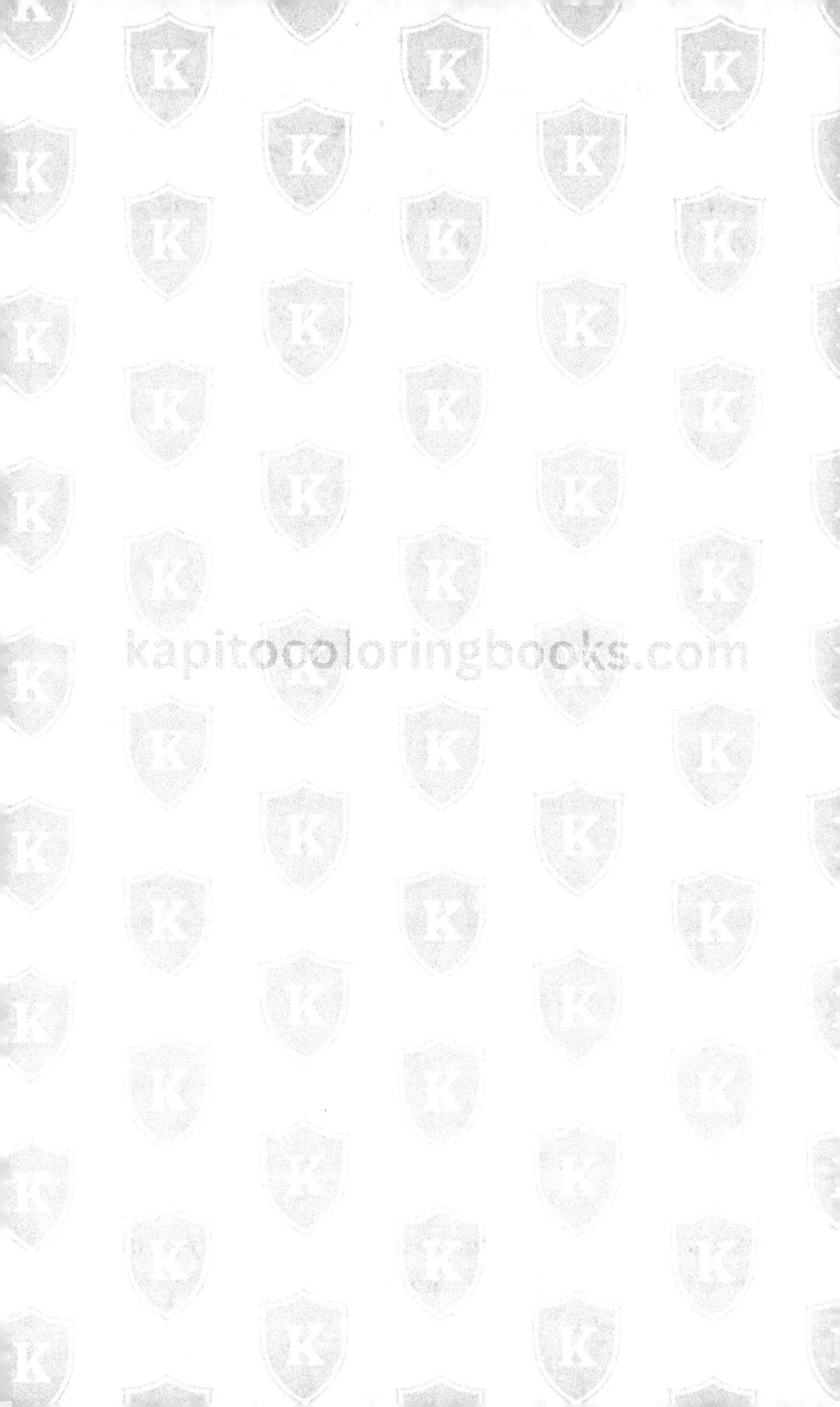

Here's a very cozy quilt, with some missing squares.
Fill in the blank squares however you'd like, then
color in the quilt using any medium you'd like.

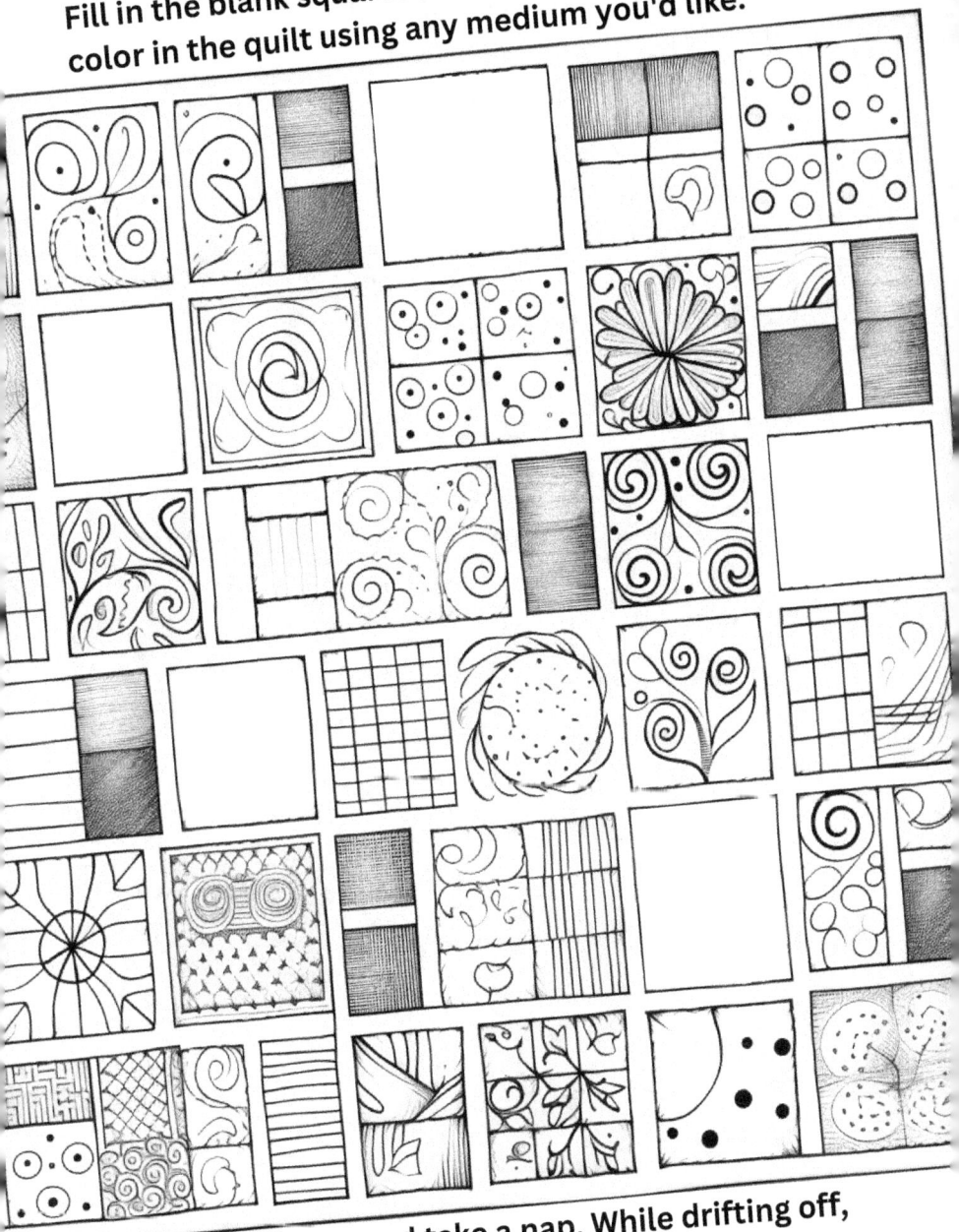

Find a nice blanket and take a nap. While drifting off,
imagine being under this quilt. Focus on all details...

What a pretty bouquet....
Draw a table for the bouquet to sit on. Perhaps a window behind the bouquet. Wallpaper? What does it look like through the window?

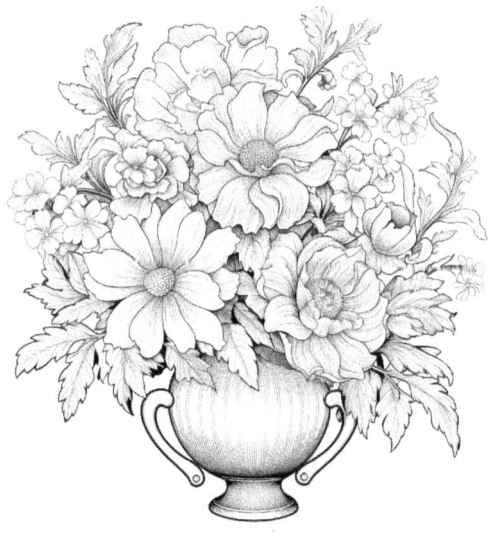

What details did you leave out in favor of others? Why?

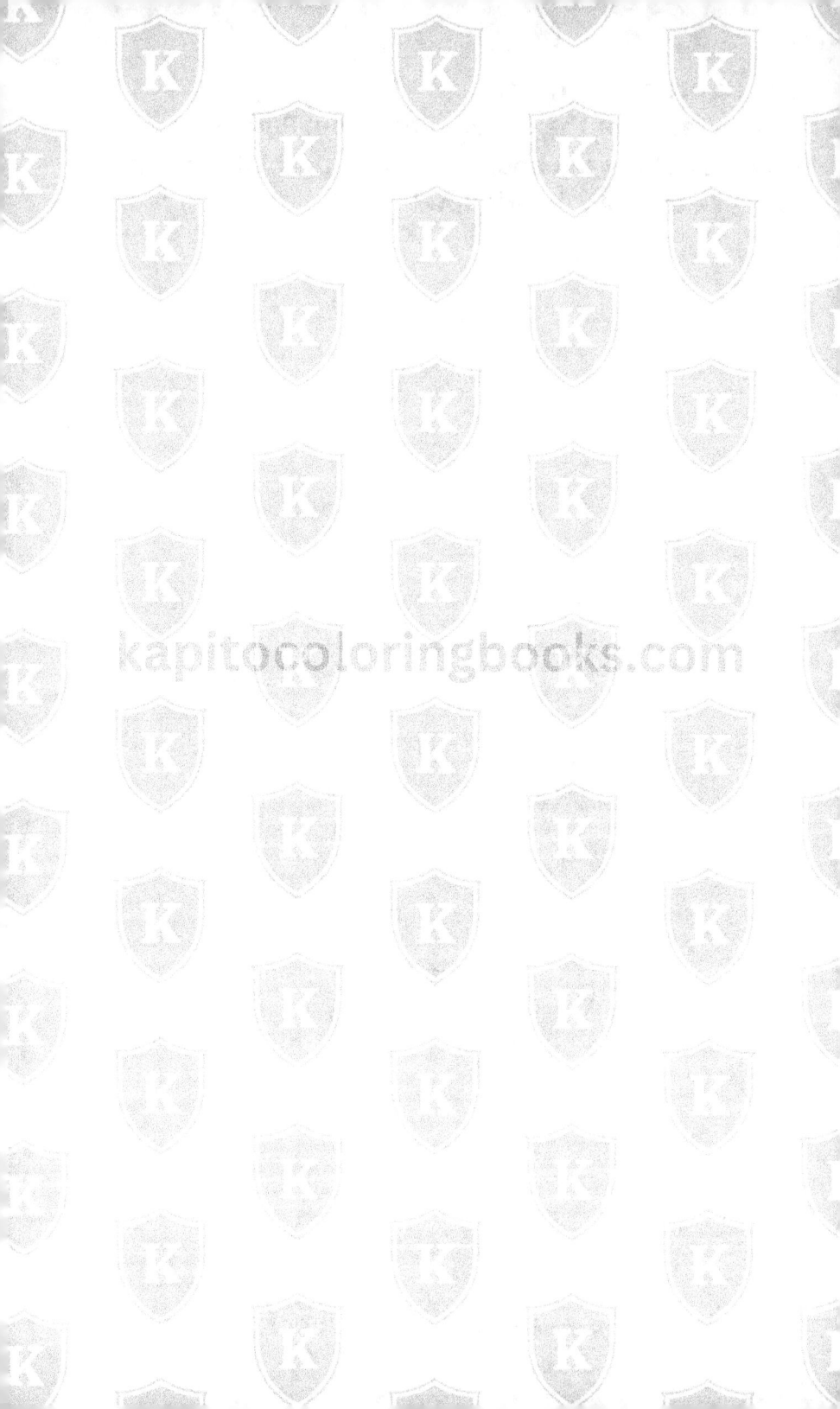

It's a beautiful day to sit and admire a city skyline, isn't it?

Wait... there's no city skyline! Please draw one. Some birds in the sky would be nice as well...

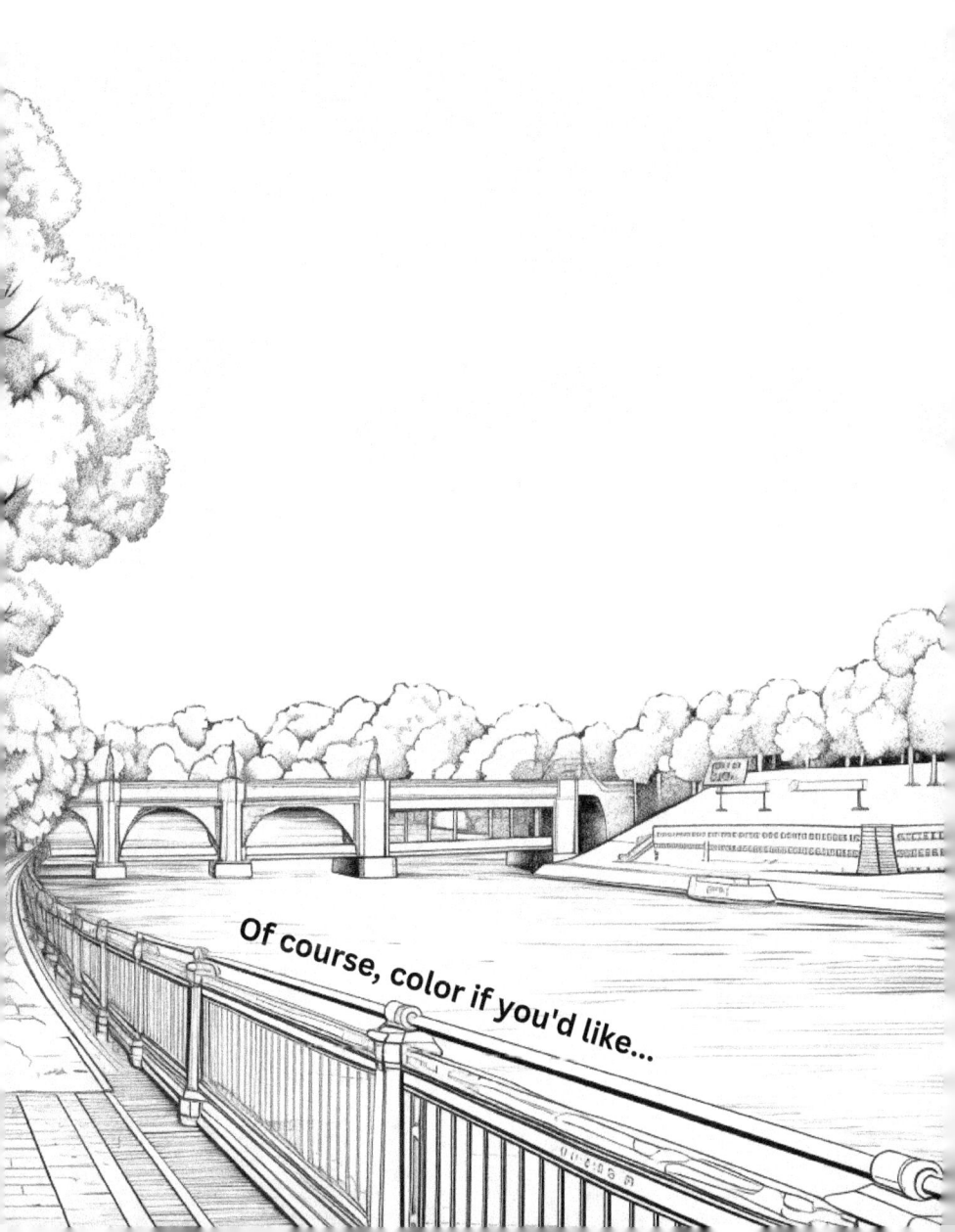

Of course, color if you'd like...

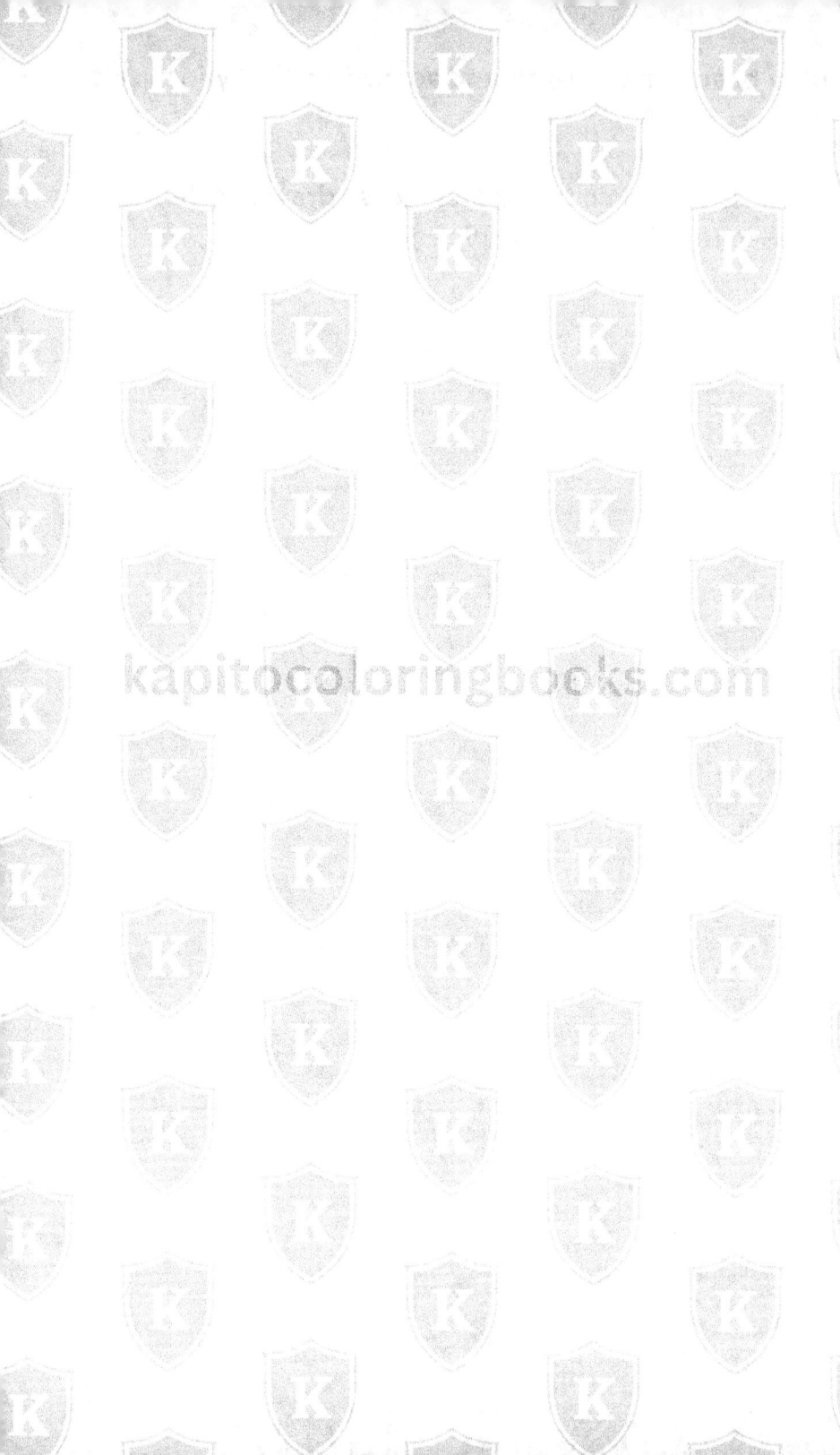

How about that time-honored artistic still life of a bowl of fruit? We've supplied the bowl, how about you draw in whatever fruit you'd like, then color or paint it all in, as well as the bowl?

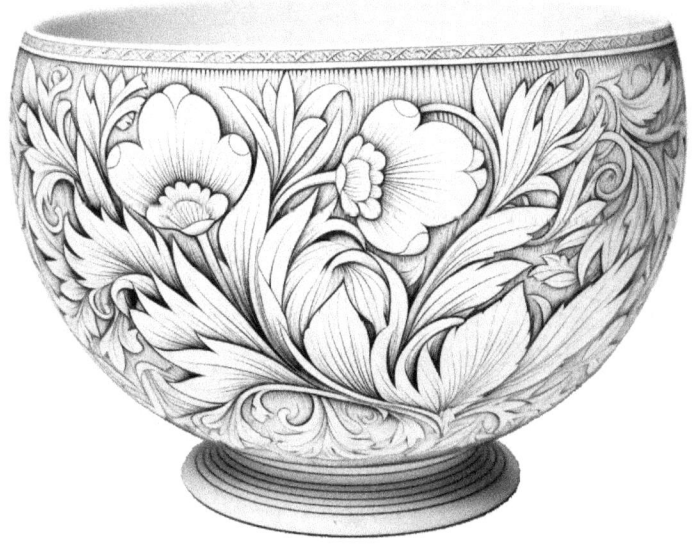

Hint.... A table might be nice too...

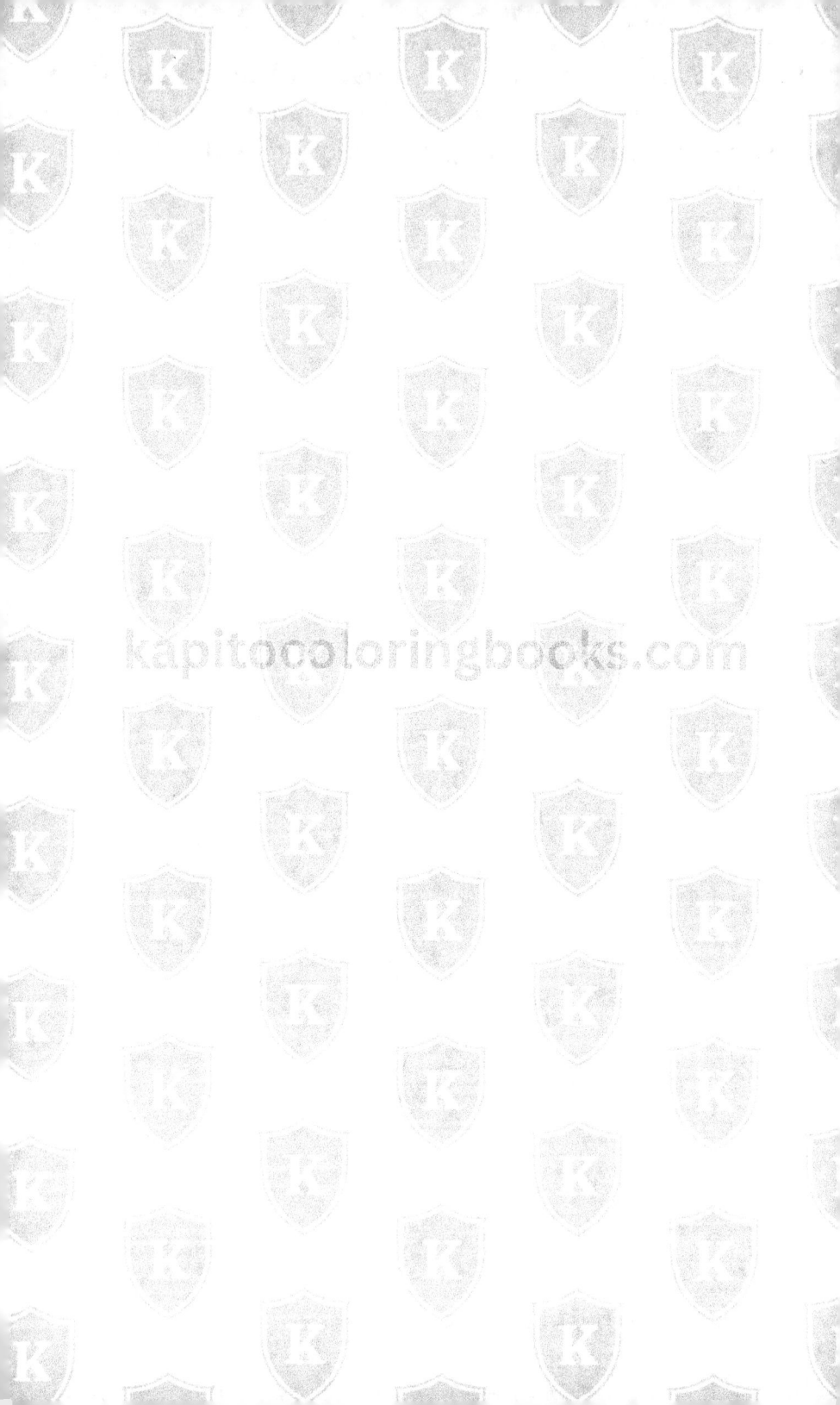

Did you know that there's a field filled with sunflower plants on the right side? There is, but you are going to have to draw it in. Then add some bursts of color!

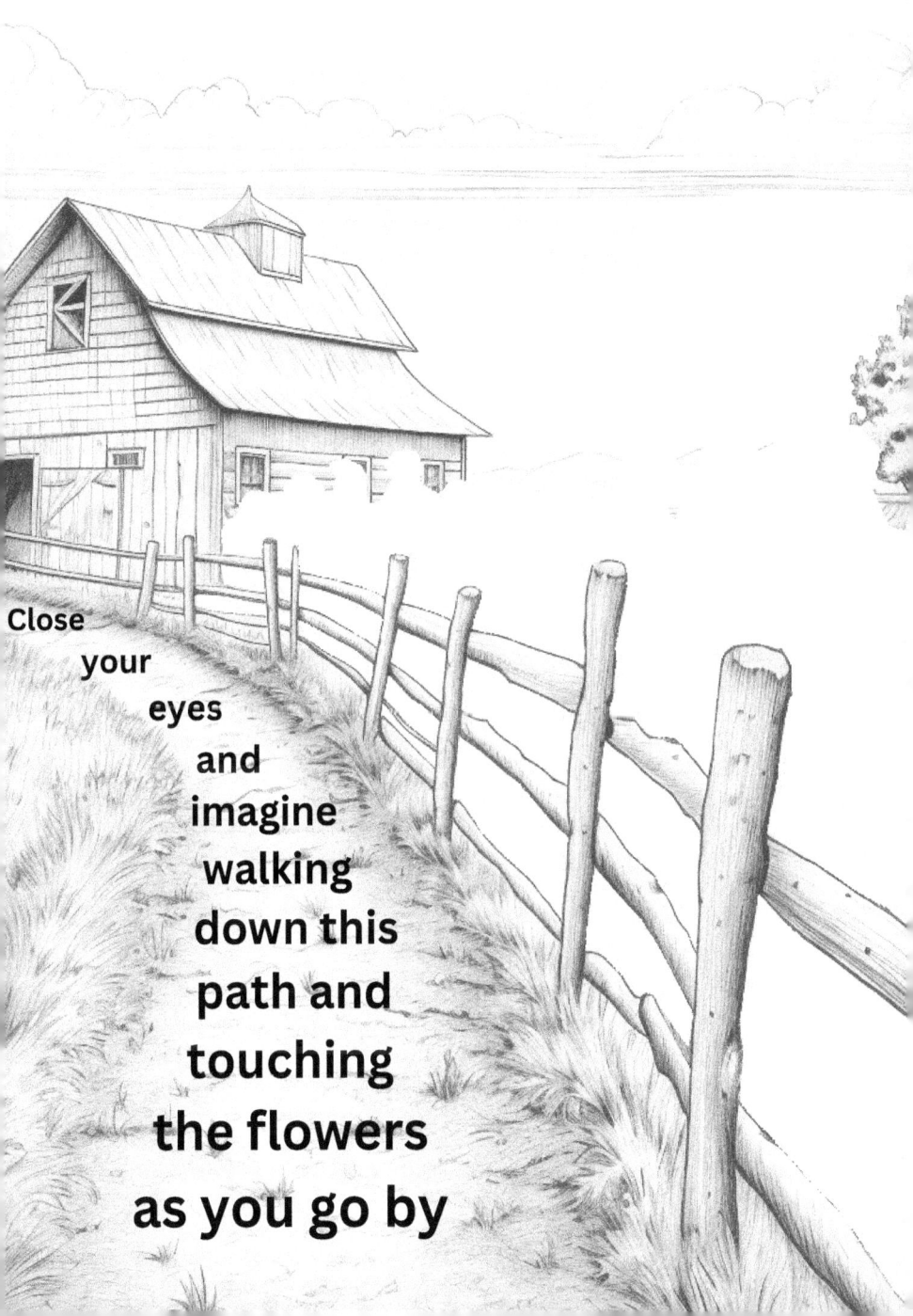

Close
your
eyes
and
imagine
walking
down this
path and
touching
the flowers
as you go by

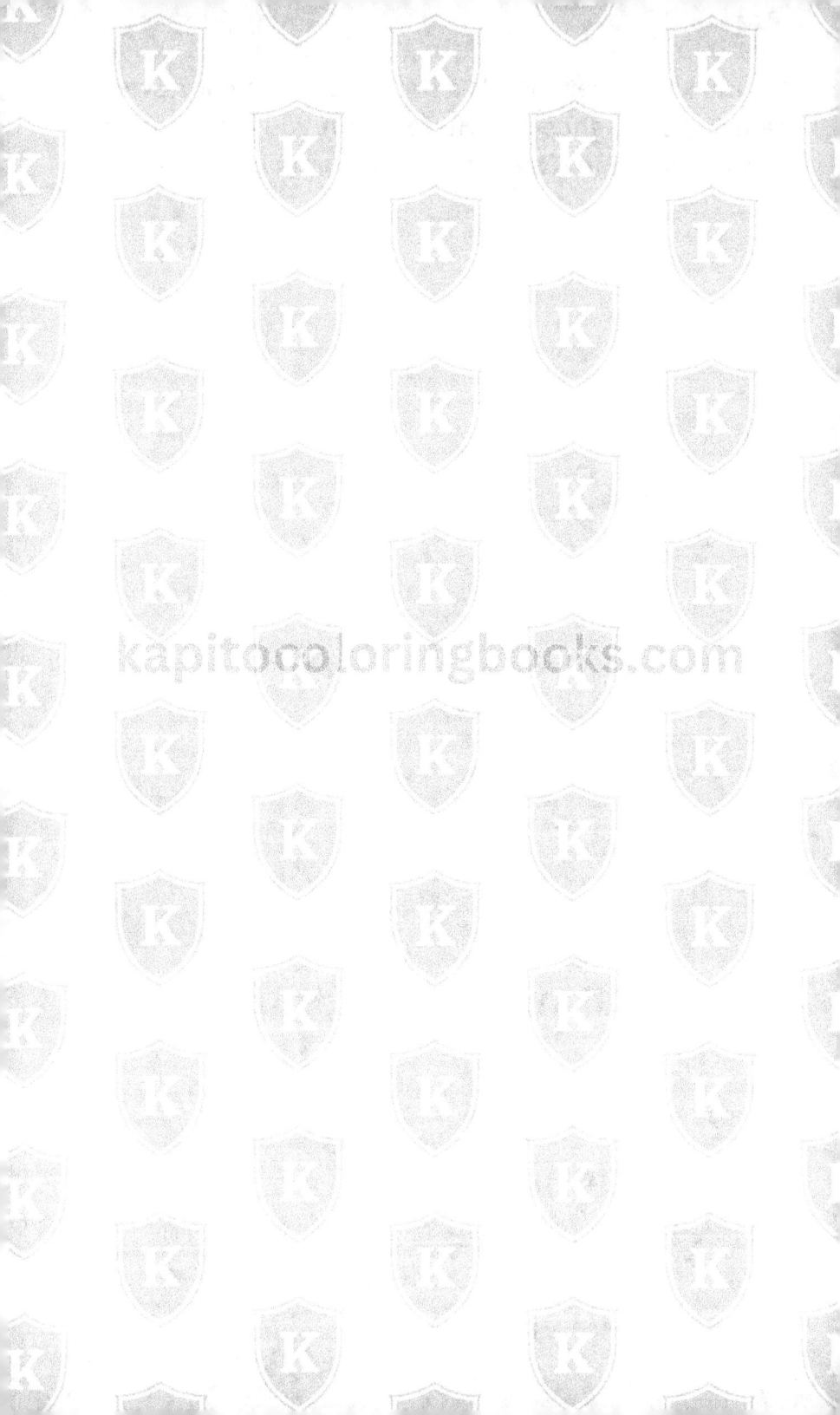

This is a cross-section of a Nautilus shell. Doesn't it look like a spiral staircase? If so, complete the floor plan of the room that leads to the stairs...

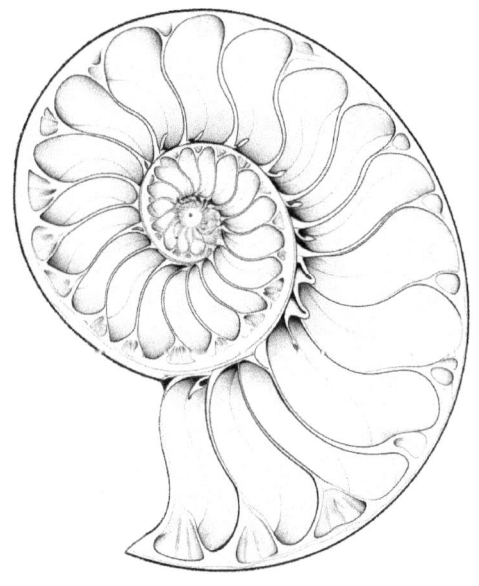

**Now imagine yourself walking down those stairs...
Where do they lead? What do you see?**

Color in this scene using only two colors. You pick the colors and you can color as lightly or darkly as you wish...

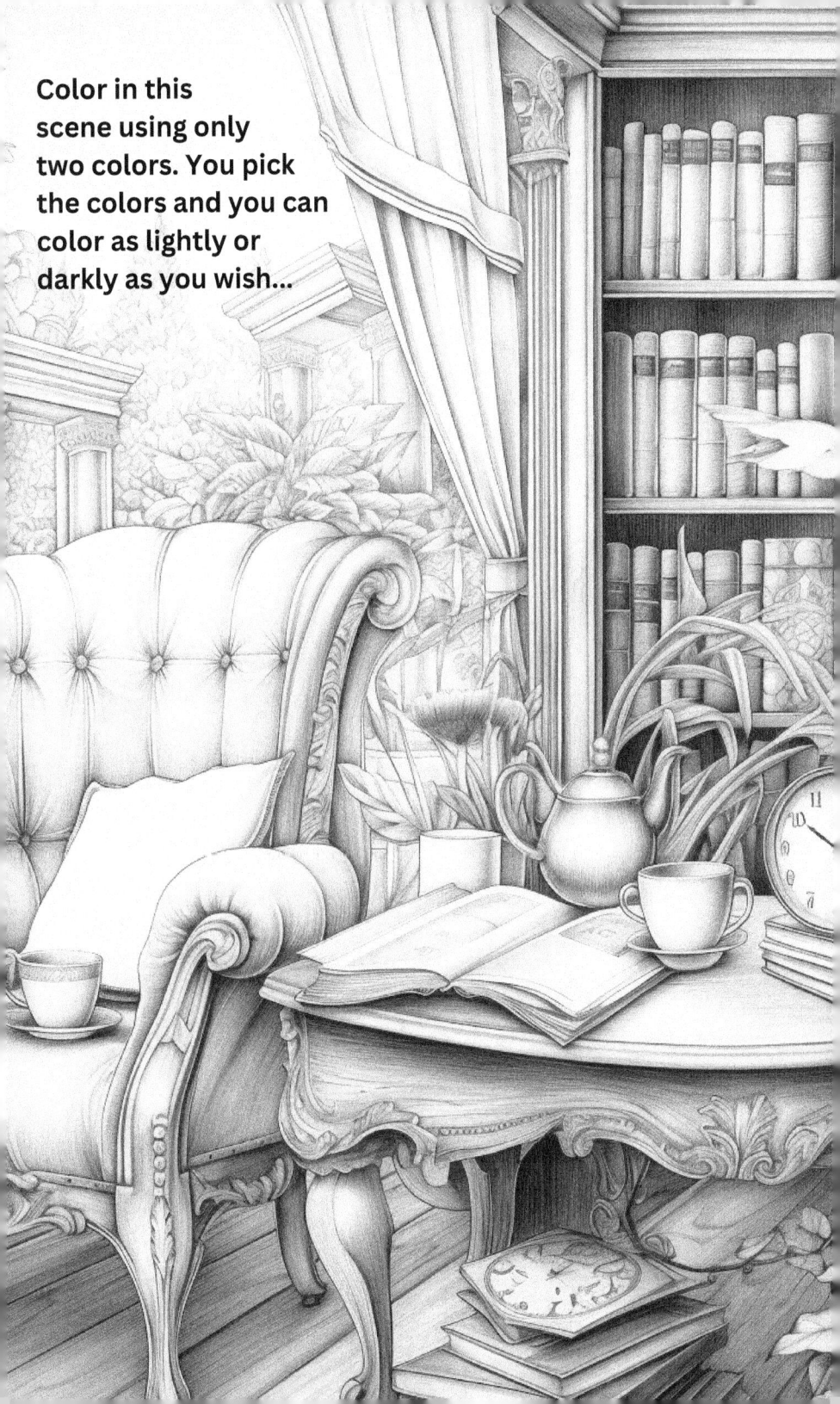

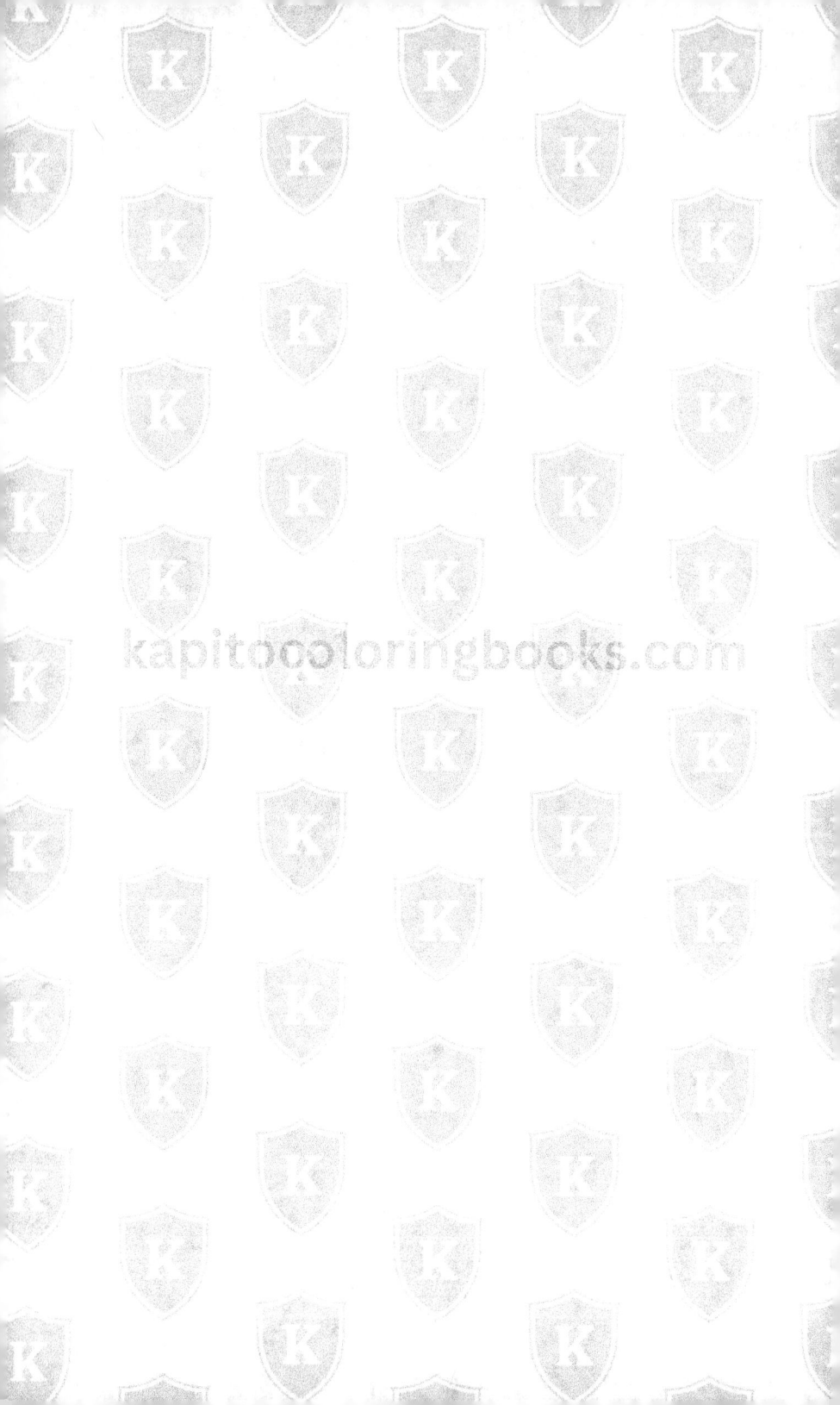

Put a pencil tip on the dot below. Close your eyes.
Draw a person riding a bicycle down a city street, in
one single, long line, without lifting the pencil. Then
open your eyes. How does it look?!?

•

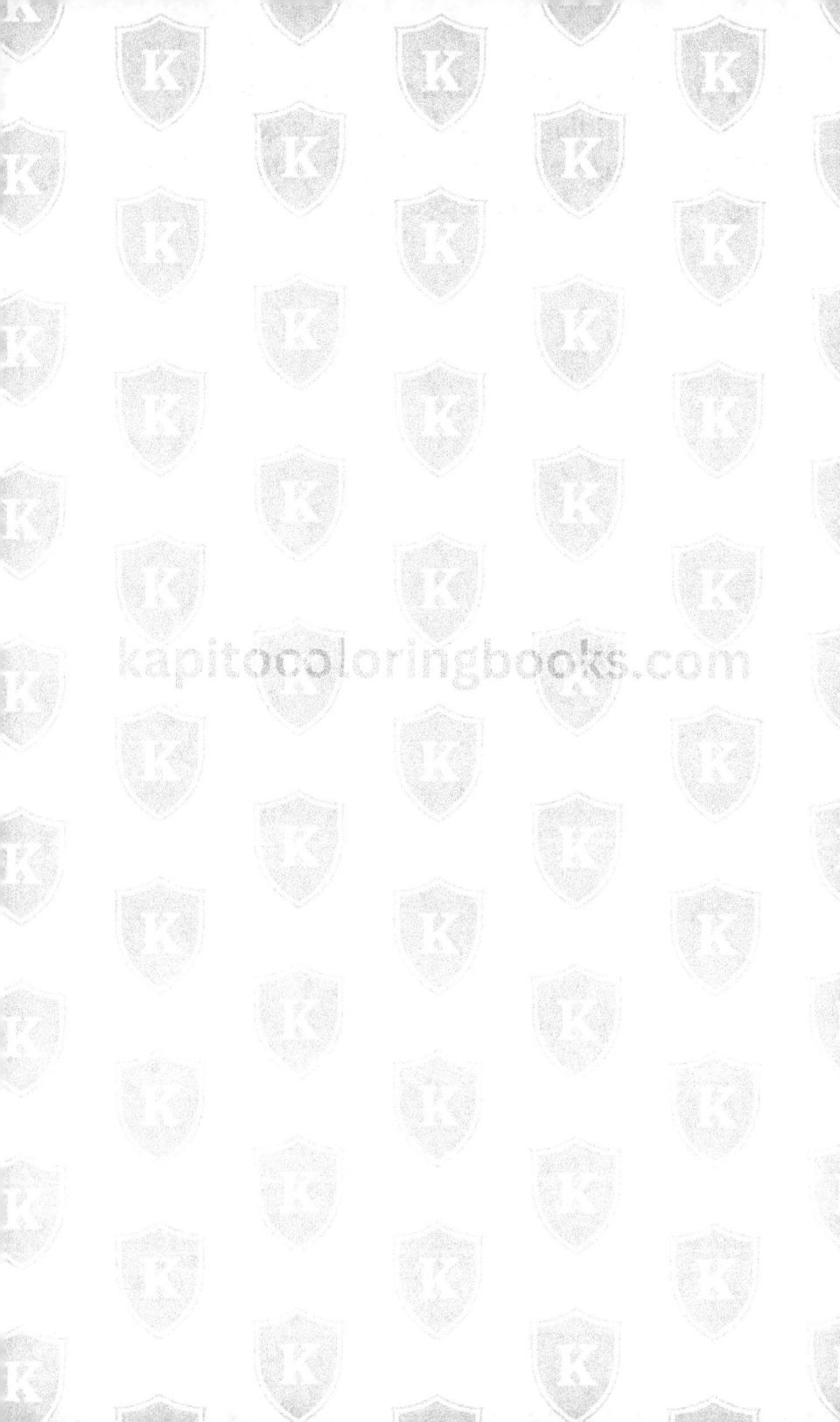

Add some fireflies to the jar, as many as you'd like, and color them brightly. Color in night-time around the children, with their faces lit up by the fireflies. Try to close in the dark as much as you can...

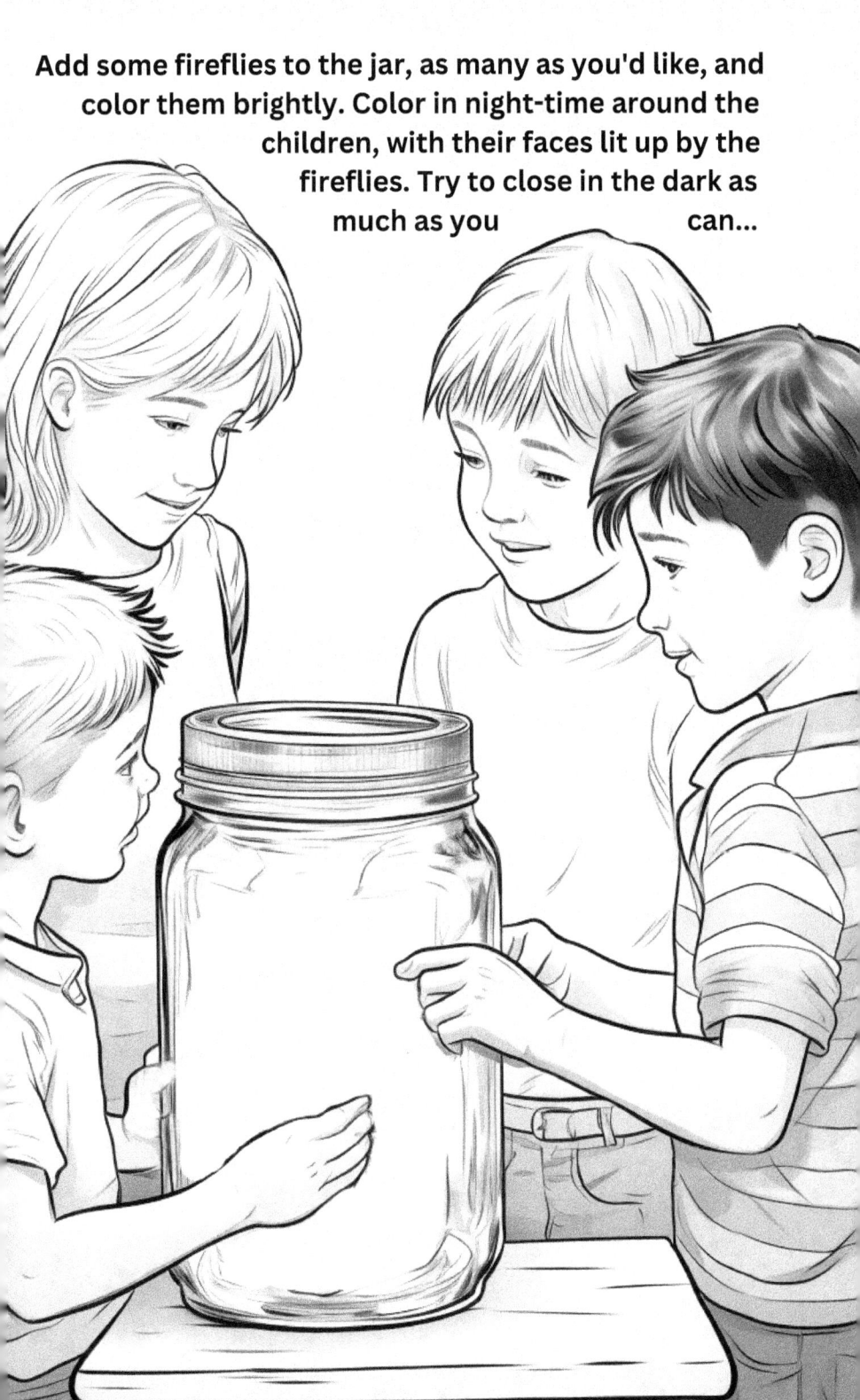

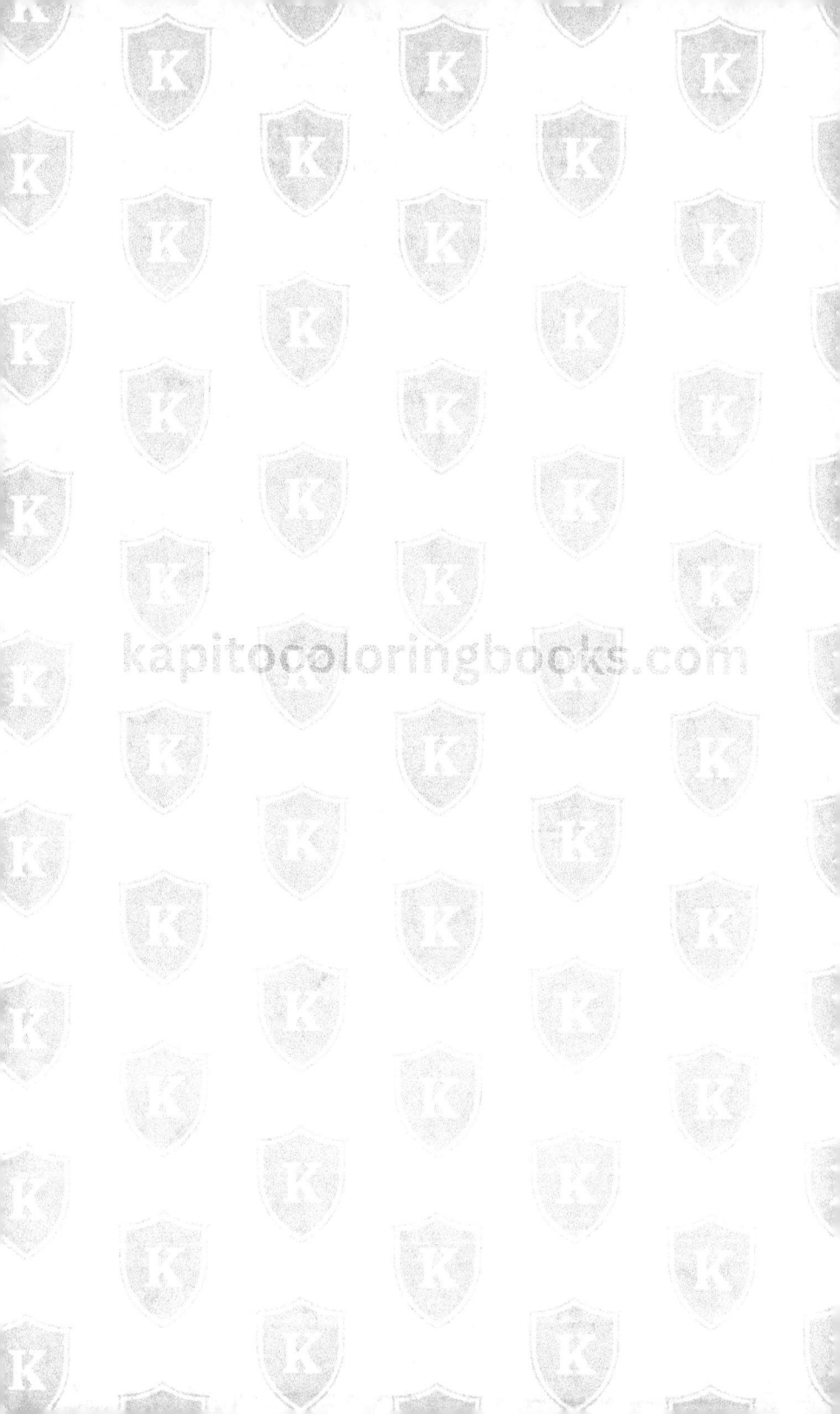

Now is your chance to let your imagination run wild, as well as a fine point marker. We've provided the shading here, but you will need to draw in the outline of a mountain landscape, with a lake somewhere in the middle. Maybe a cabin and a small boat...?

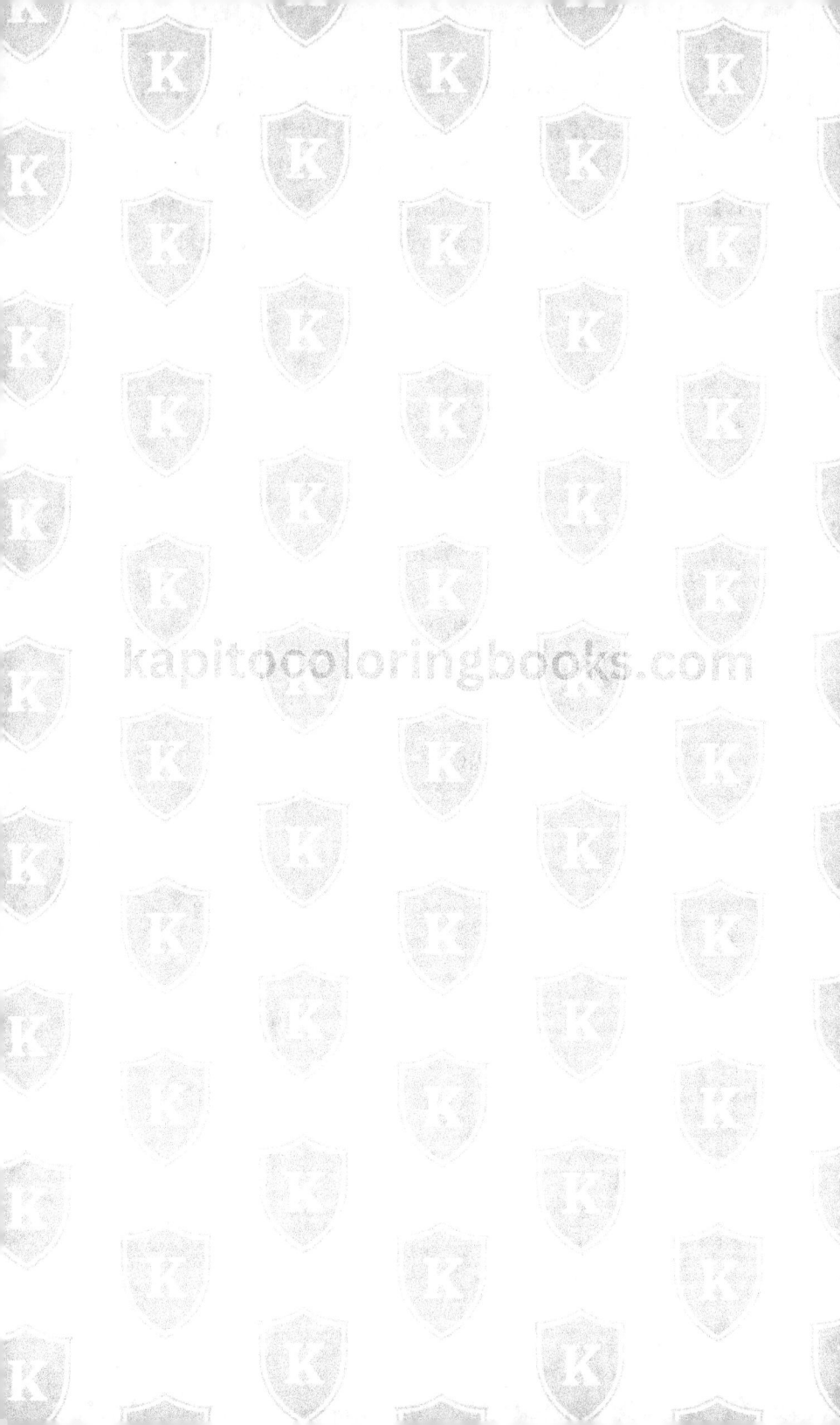

This one is easy. Just turn off your brain, and color these beautiful butterflies...

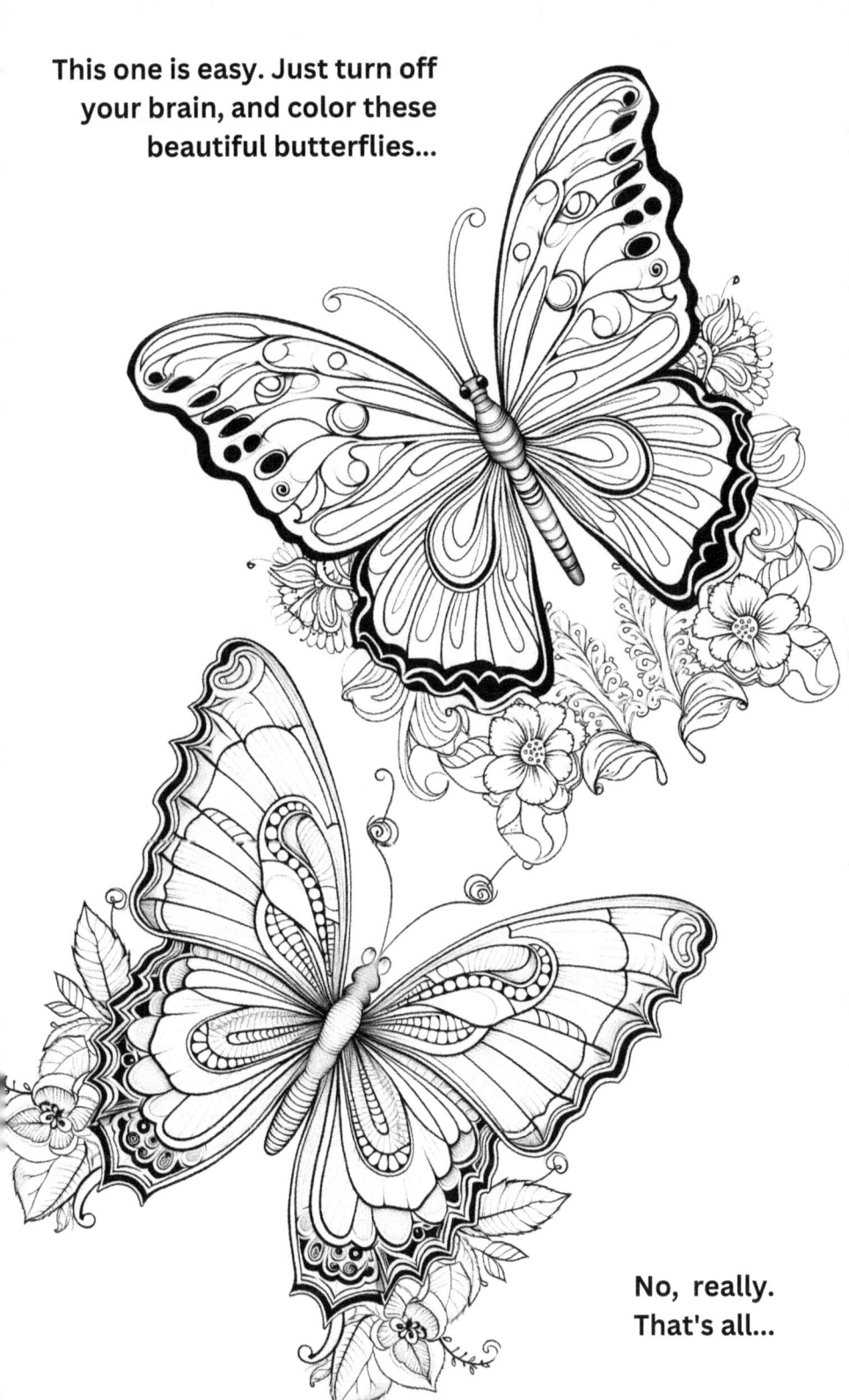

No, really. That's all...

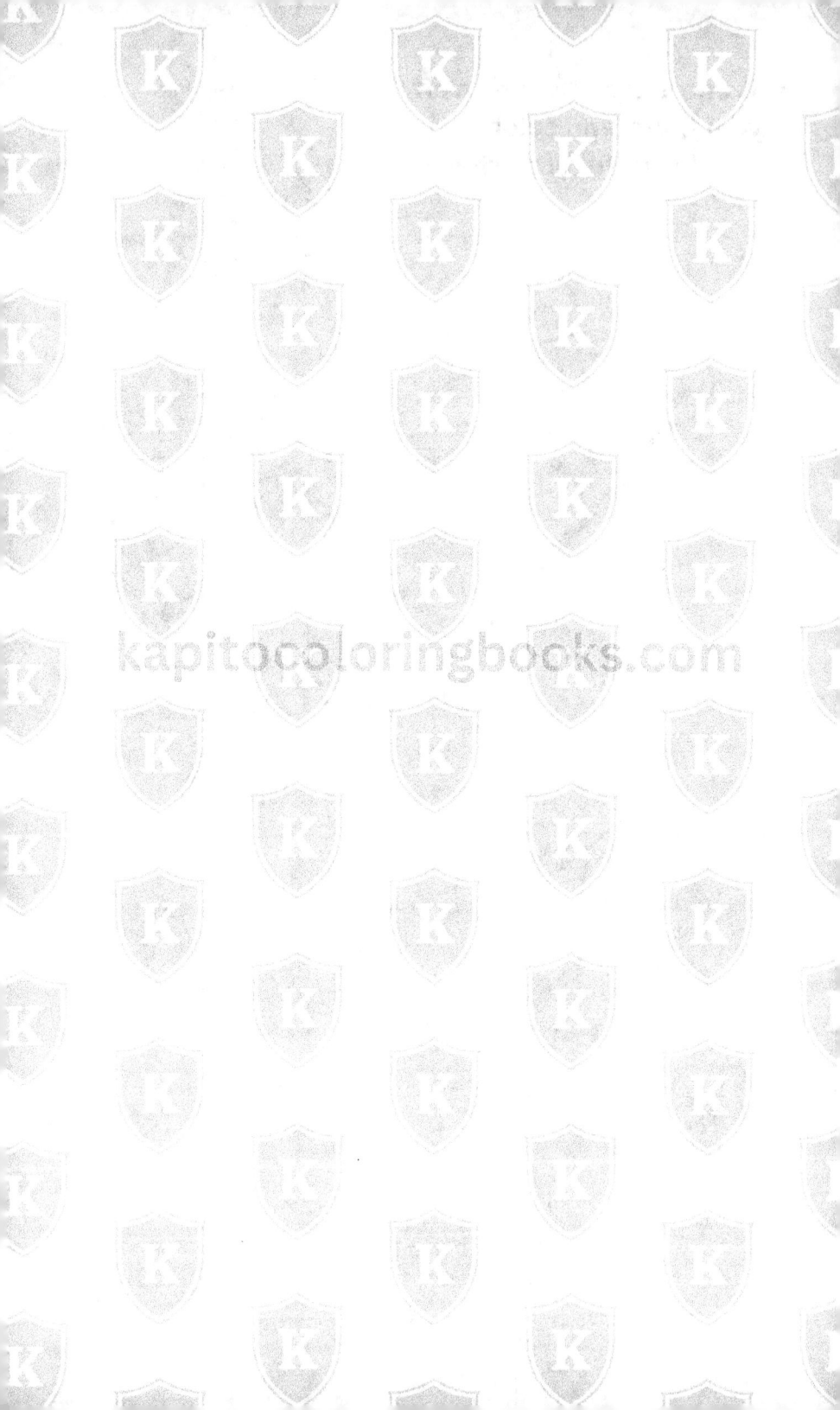

See the maple leaves hanging out below? Using the ones you see as a guide, draw more maple leaves in piles to fill the page. Choose a season to color them.

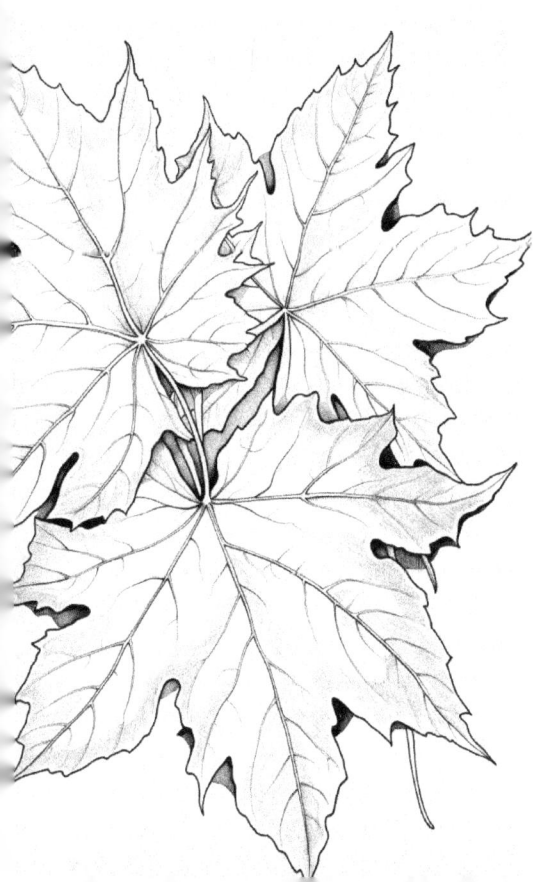

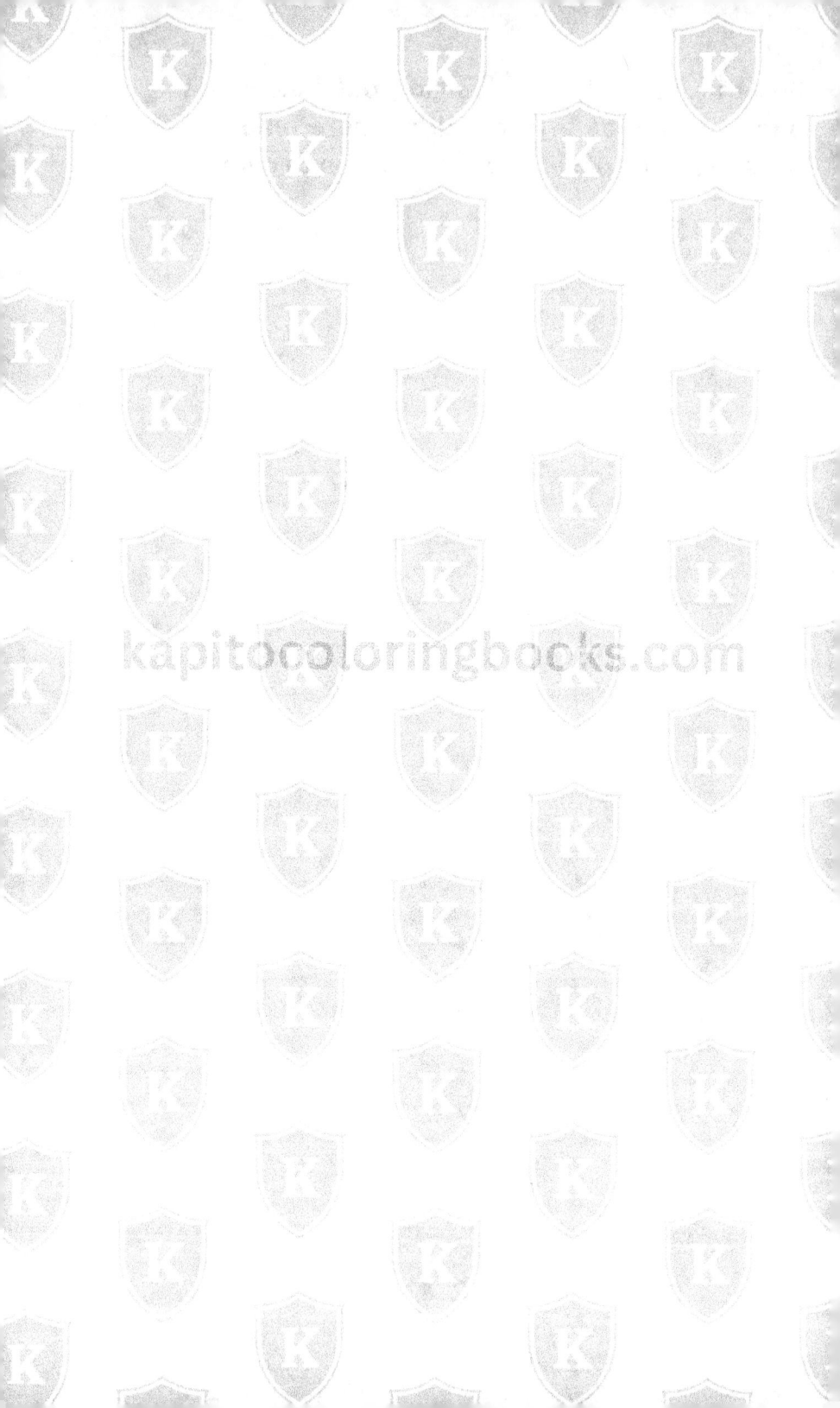

Below is a vintage camera with a big old fashion-ey flash bulb on top. Draw someone standing behind it and holding it, to take a photo. Draw a background too.

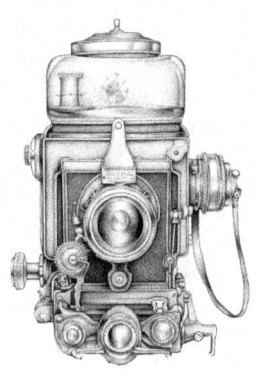

Did you draw someone old fashion-ey as well? Or a modern person? Why?

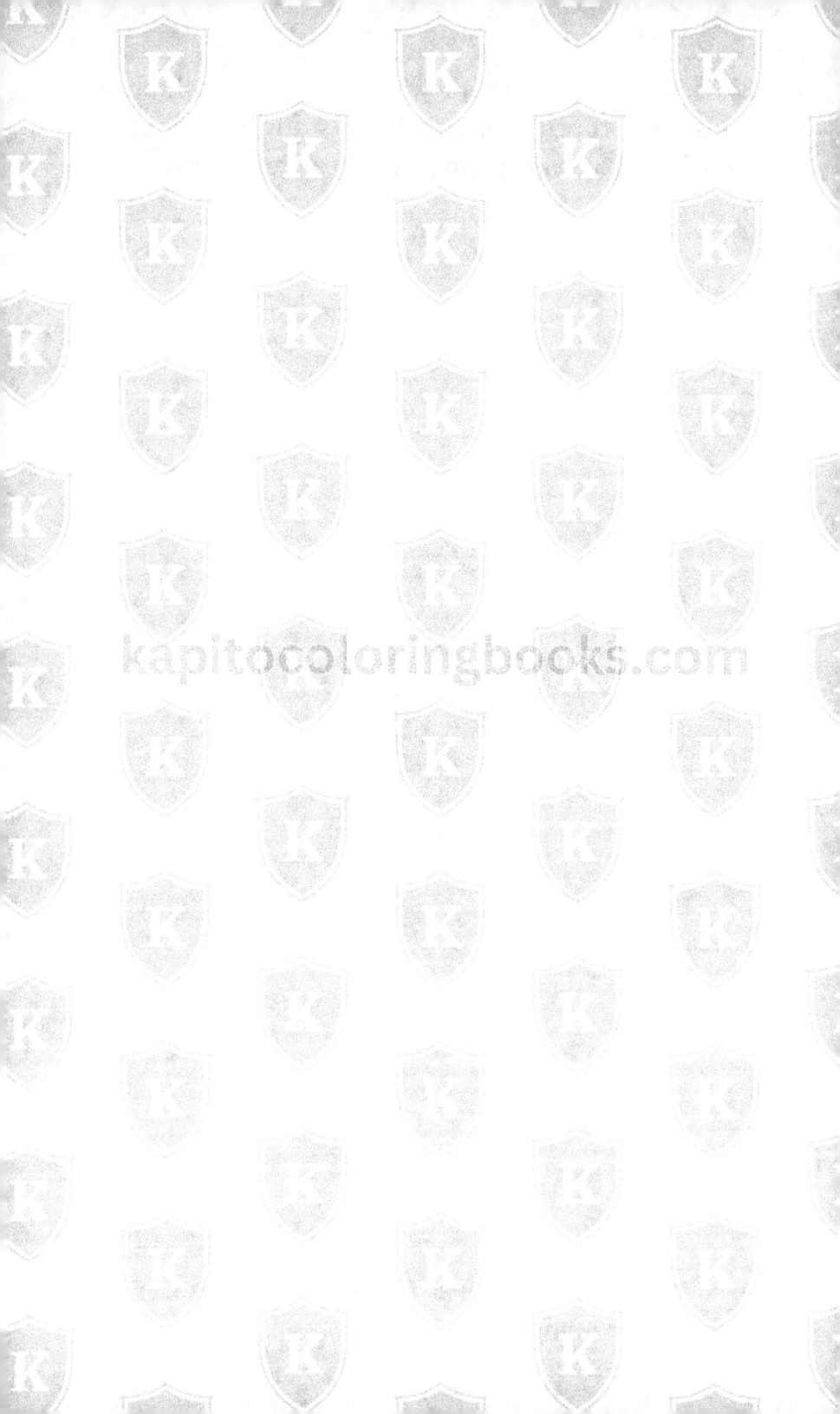

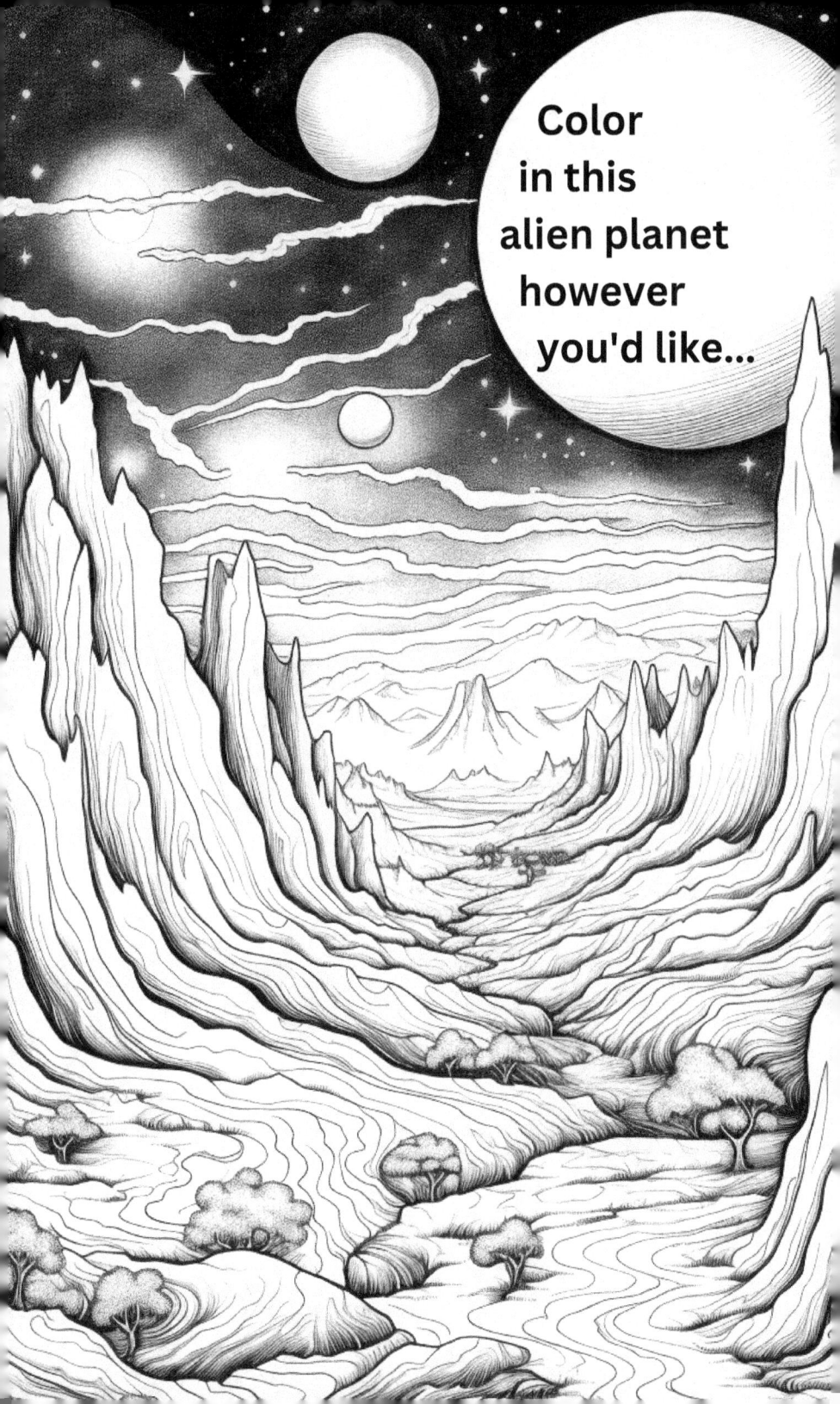

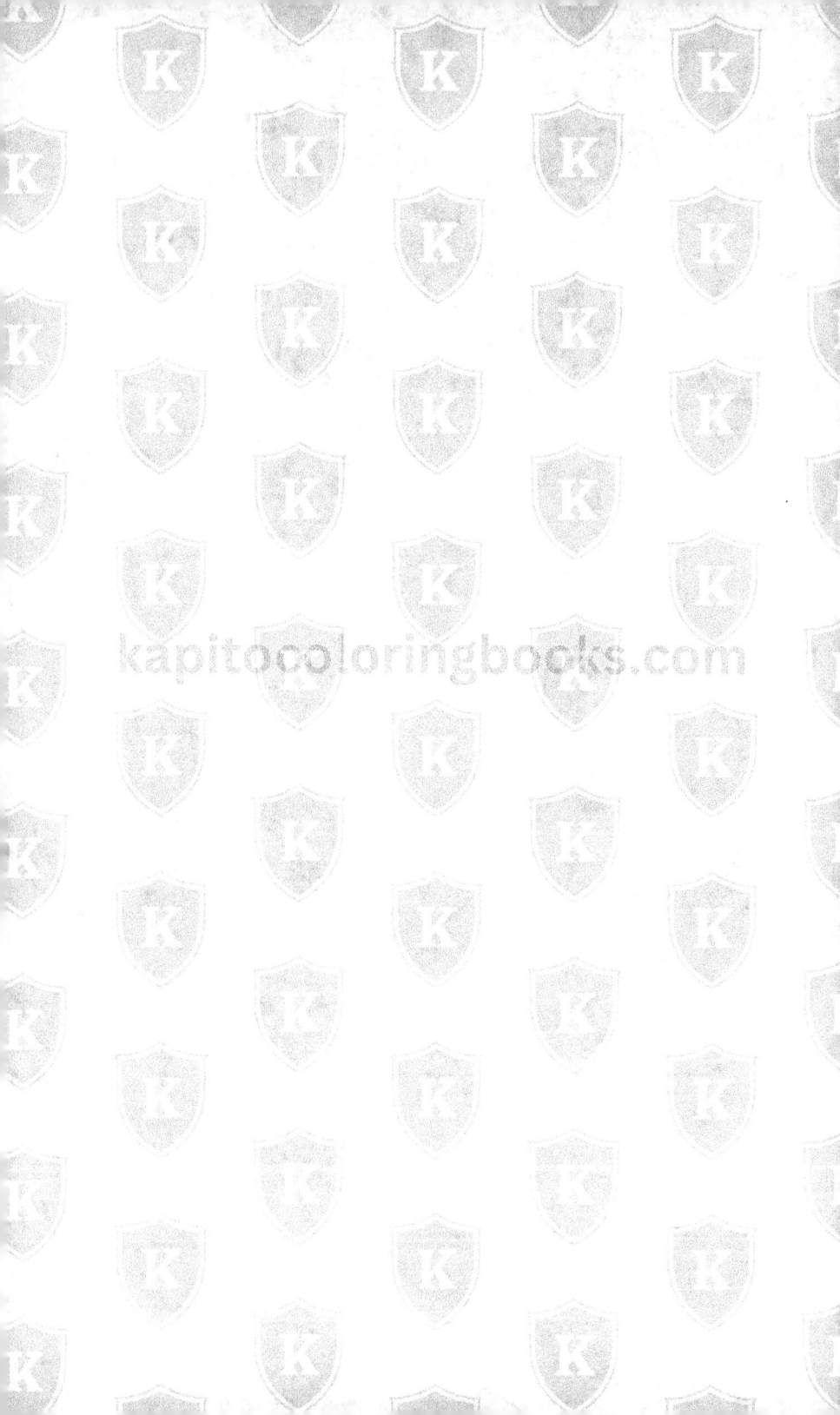

Find a feather and put it under this page. Using a pencil, rub this page to get an outline of the feather. Draw in outlines and color.

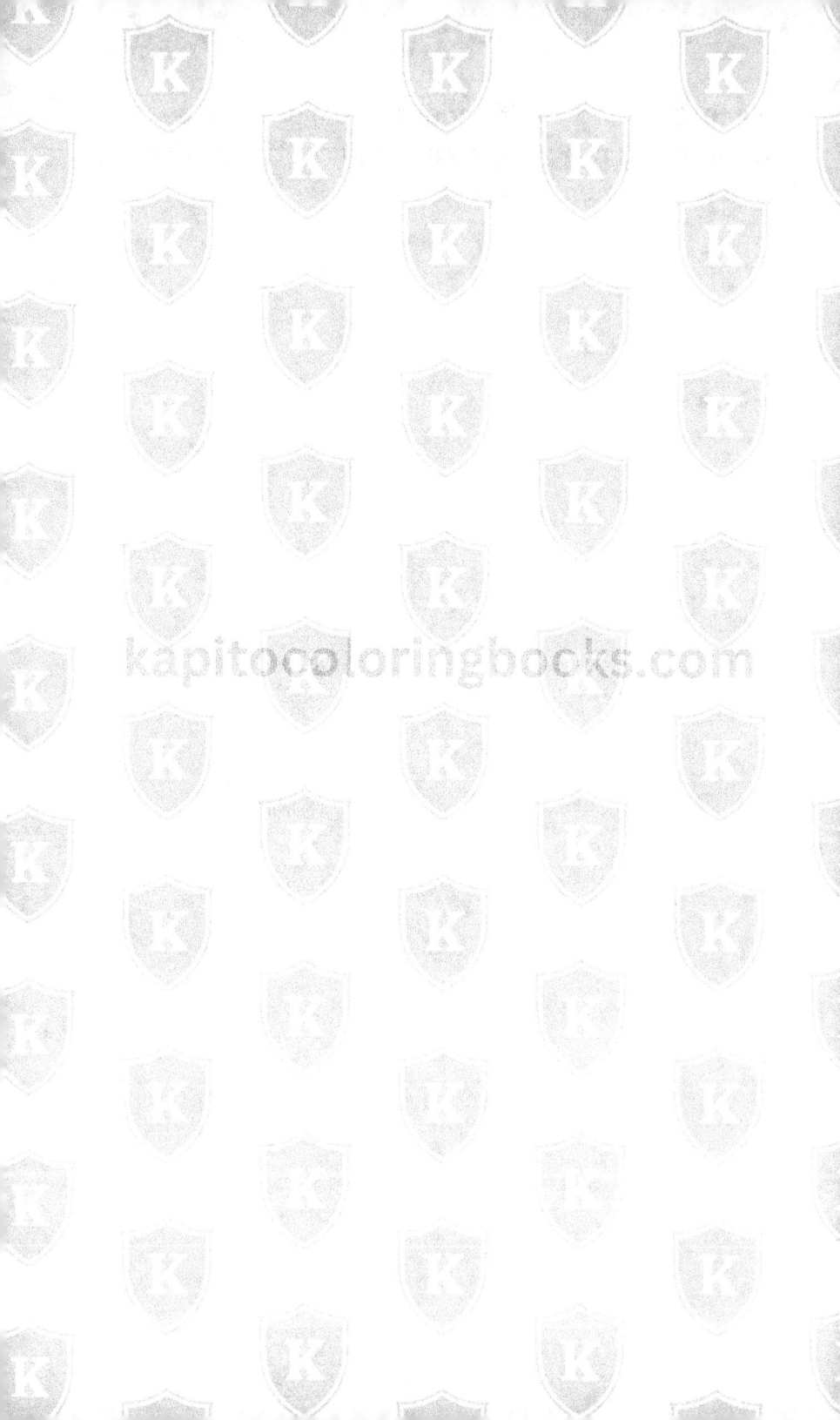

Draw a lighthouse in the background, and color everything in...

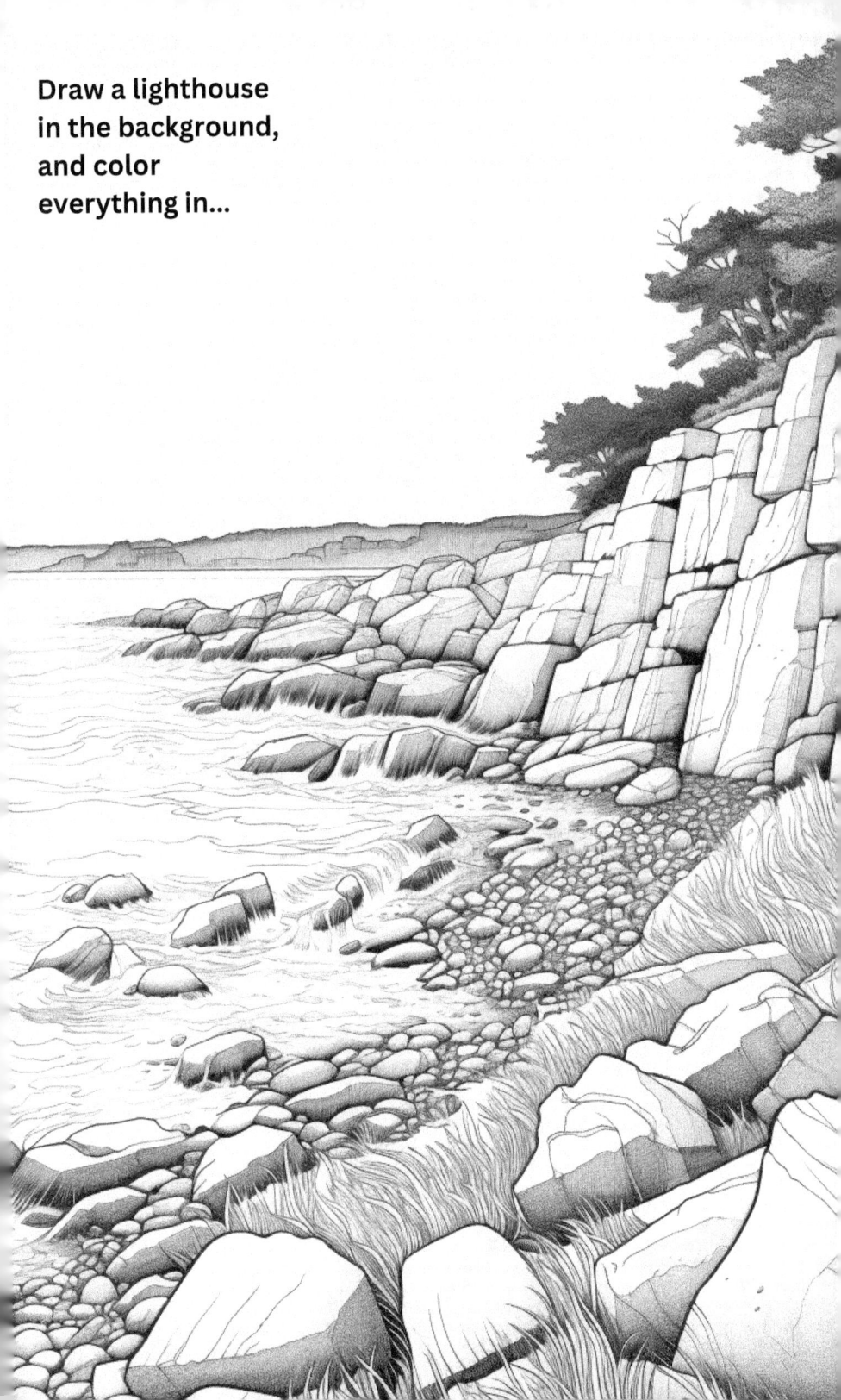

The dragon looks kinda angry... Draw a castle on the side of the mountain. Let's hope he doesn't destroy it!

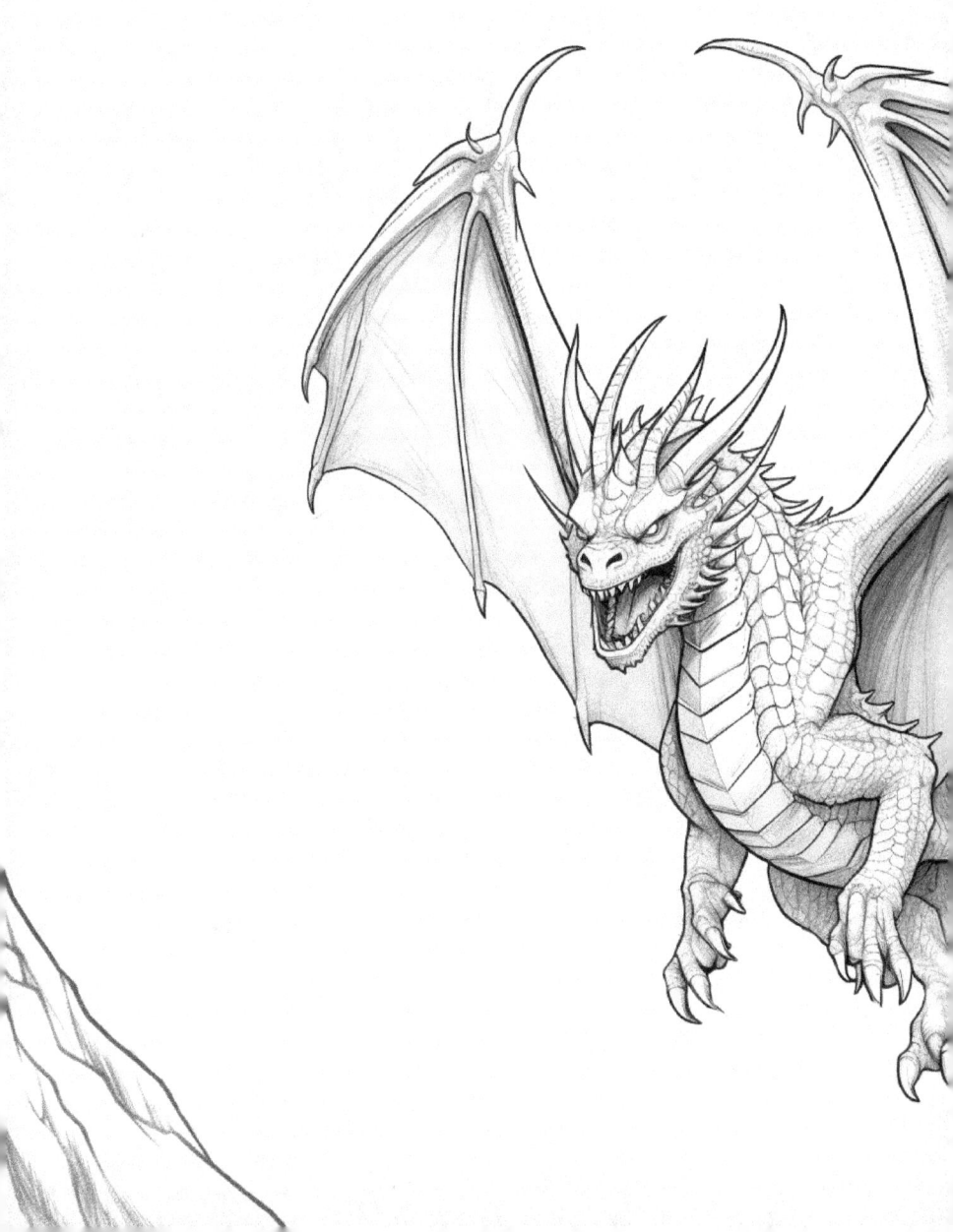

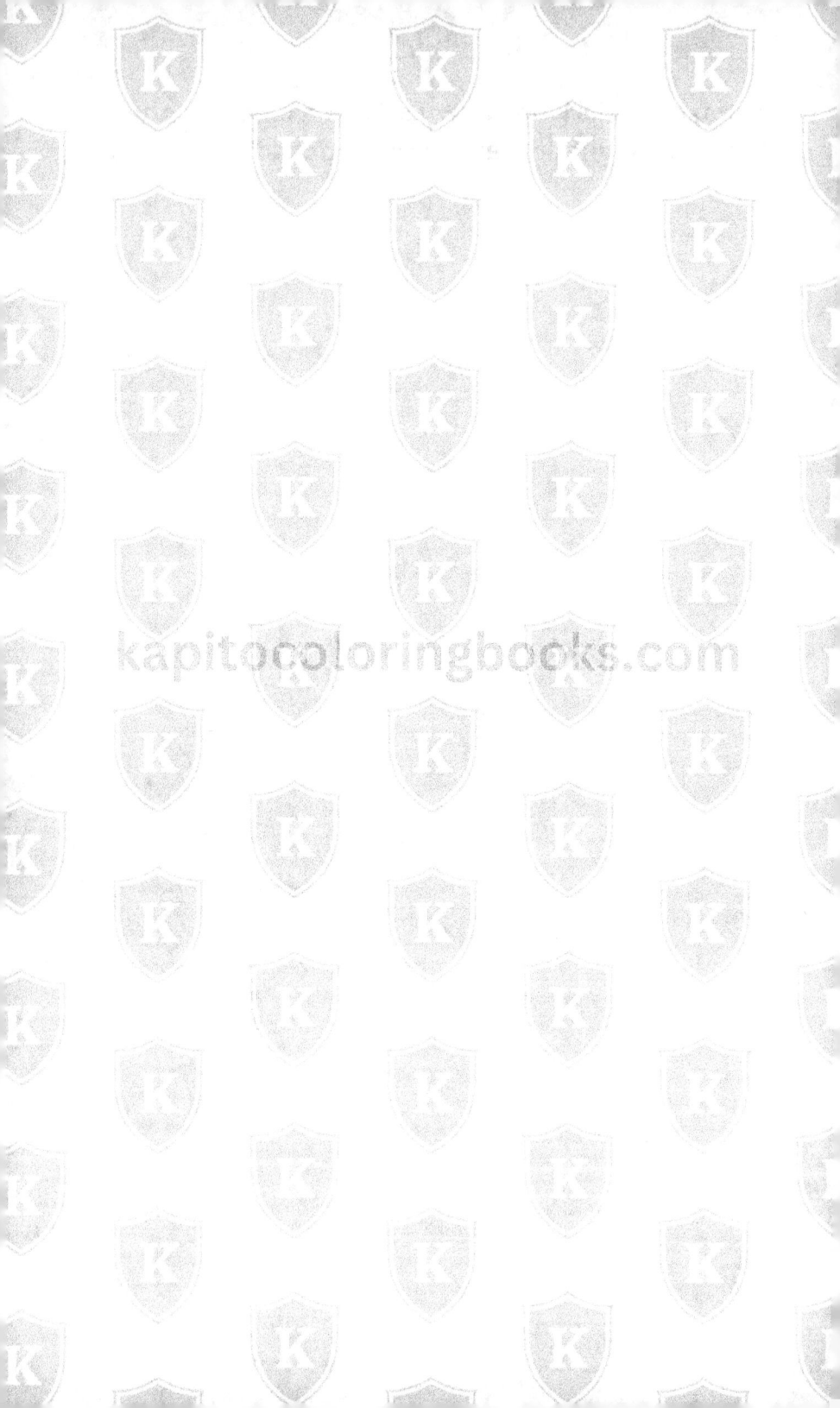

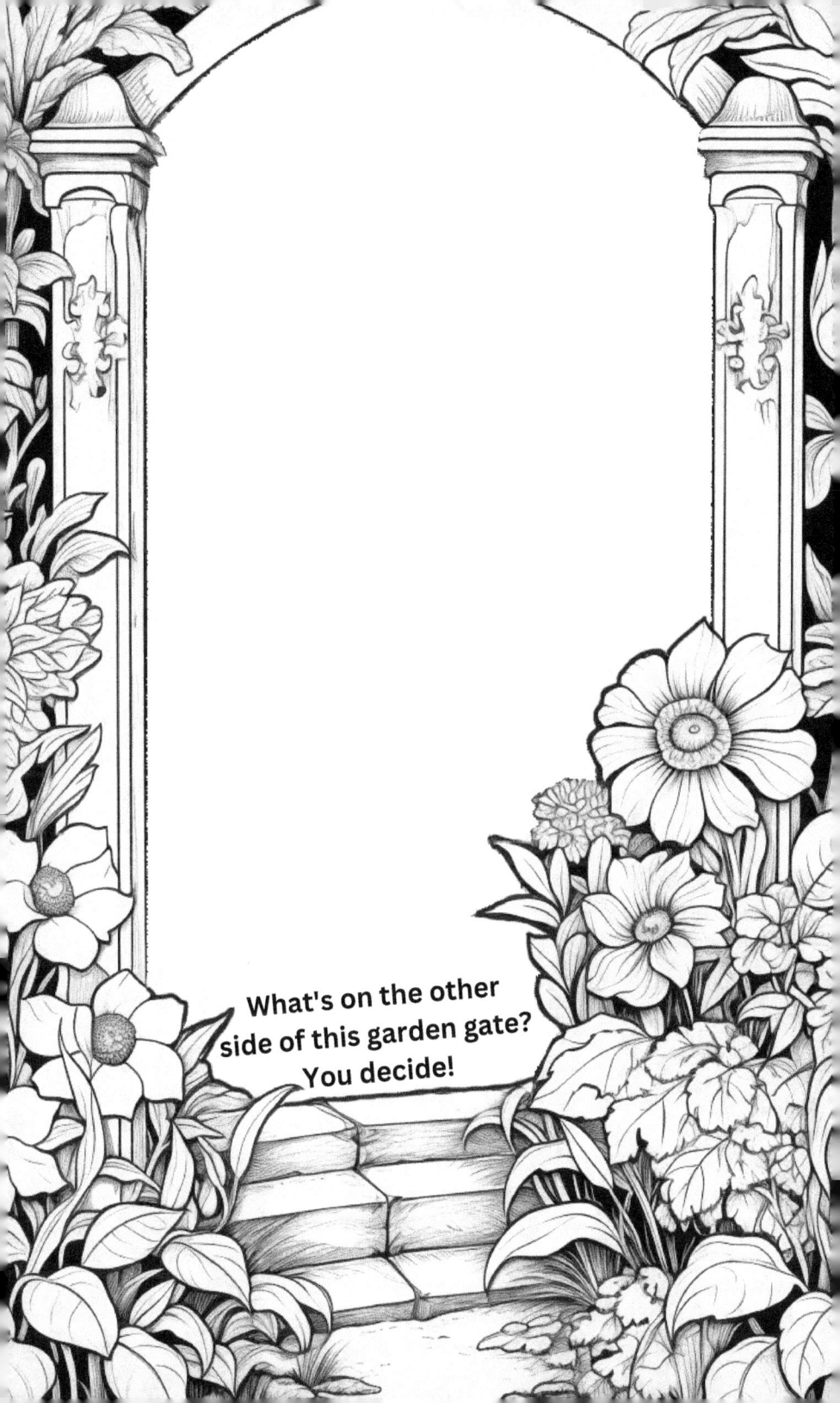

What's on the other side of this garden gate? You decide!

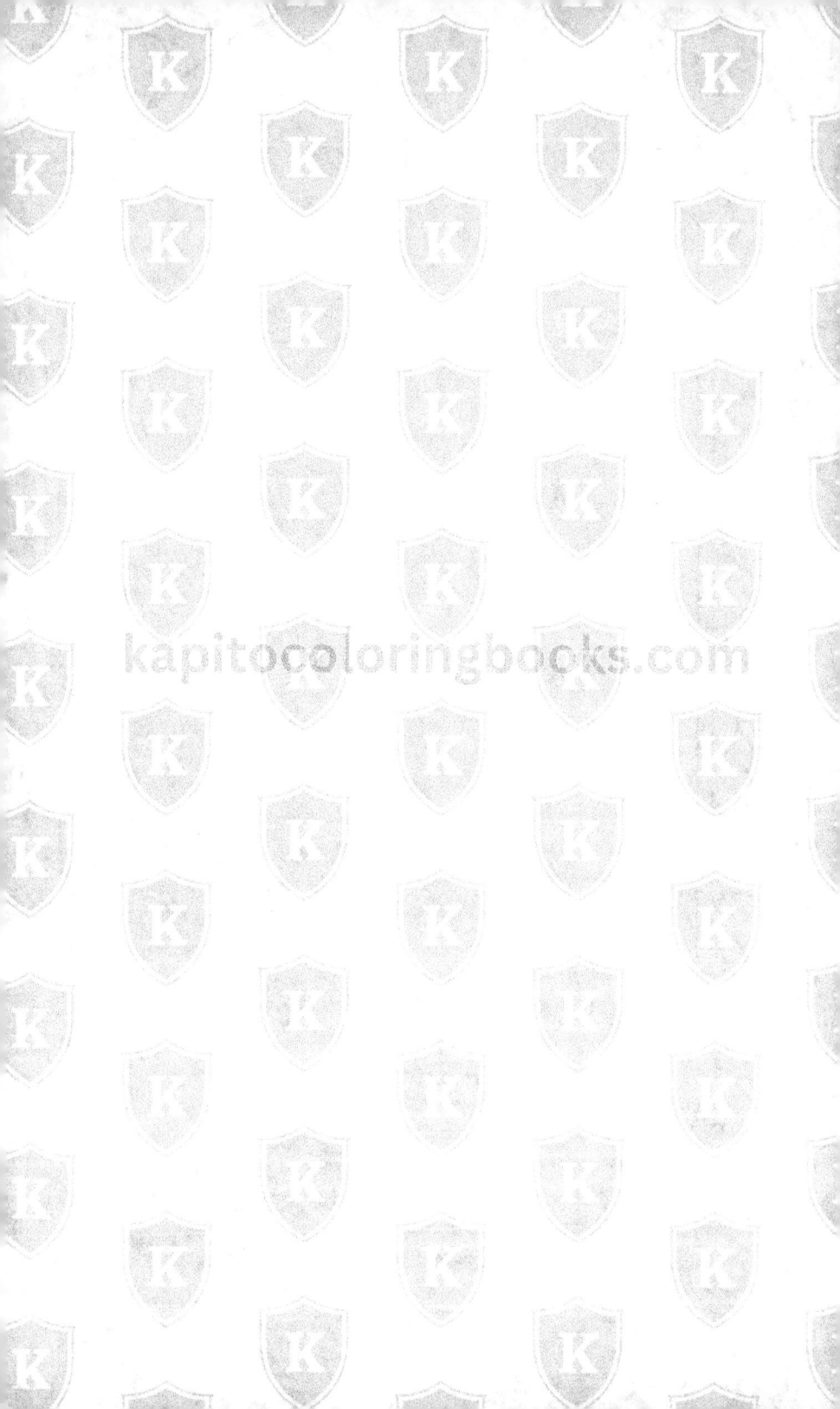

This forest path needs a forest. Please draw in a nice, dense forest on both sides of the path. Remember to use perspective as the path goes on into the distance.

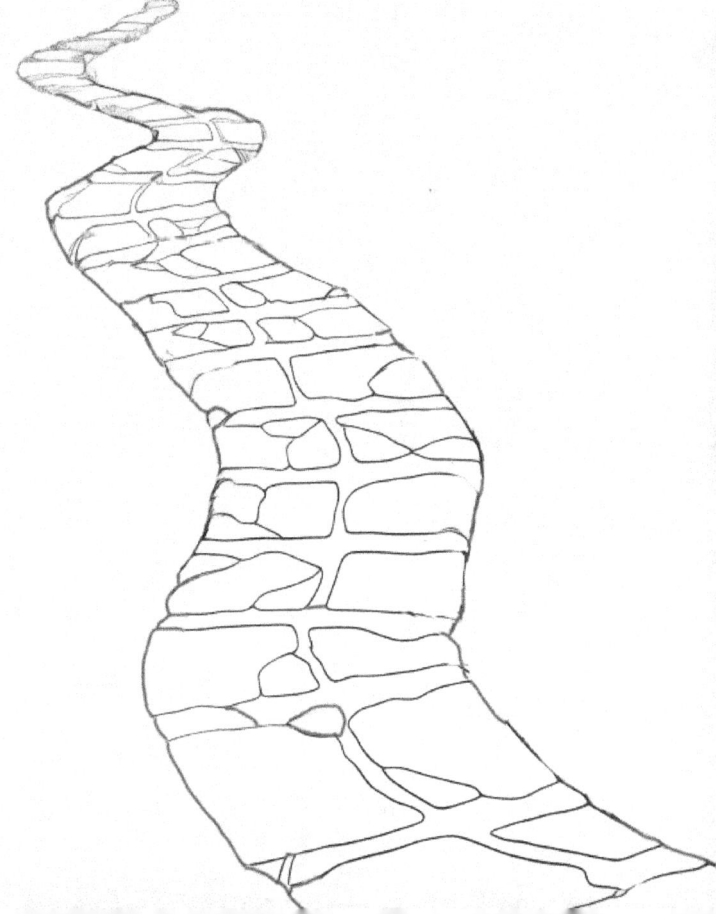

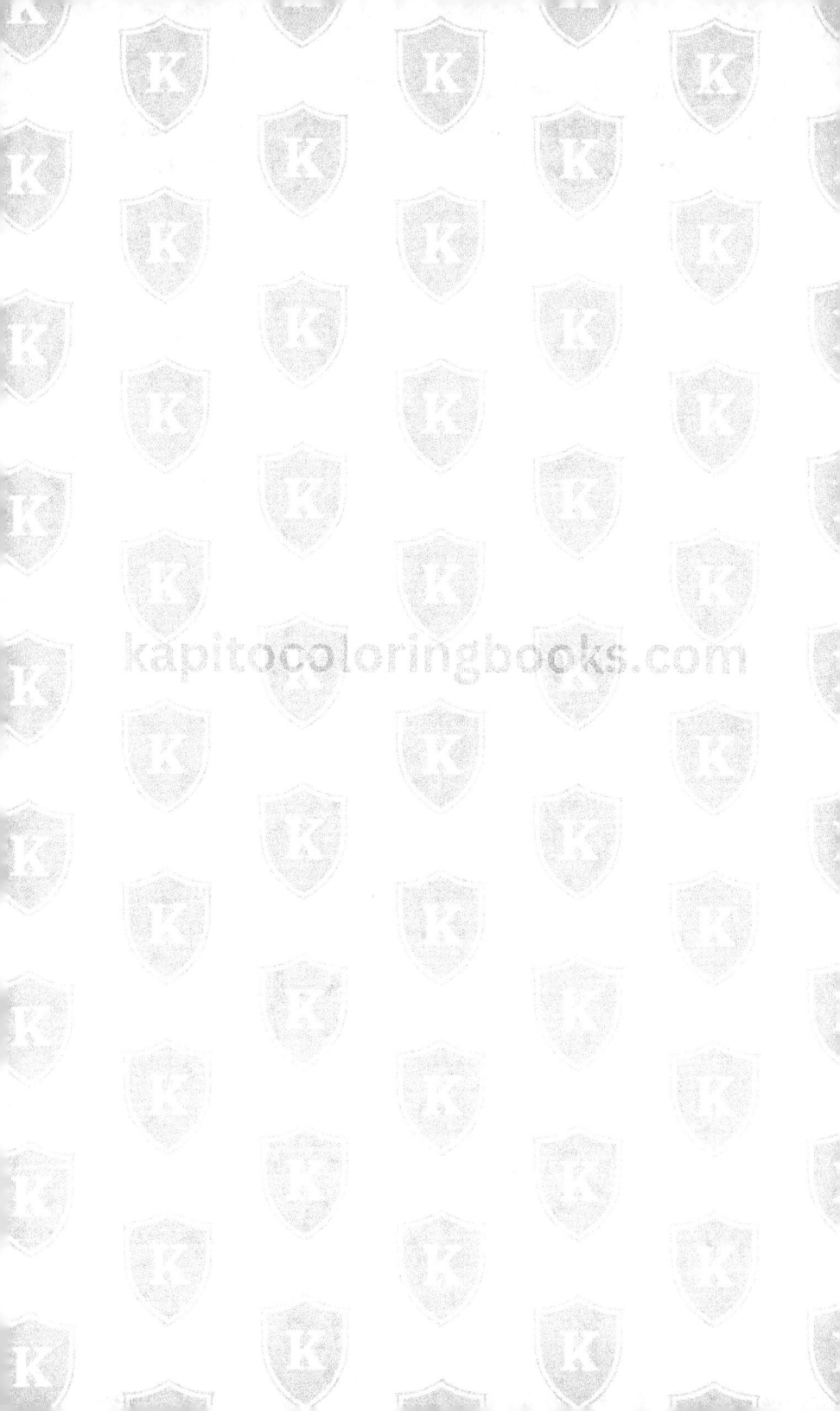

Here's a pair of sneakers. It needs a person standing in them. Make it fun!

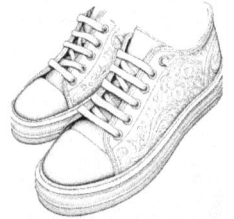

Here's a whole flock of birdhouses, ready for you to color.
But before you do, how about drawing in a bird or two?

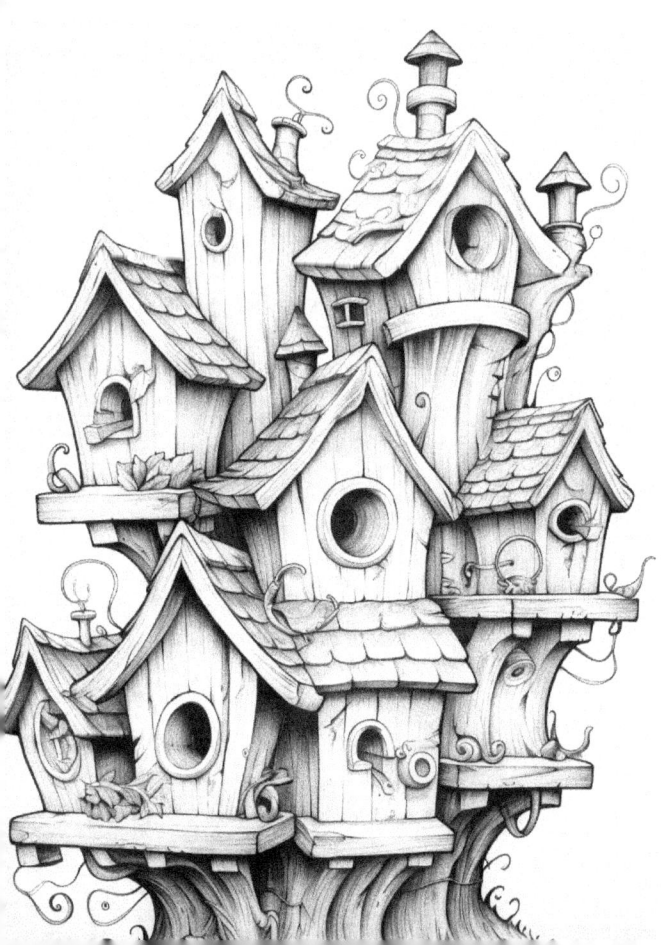

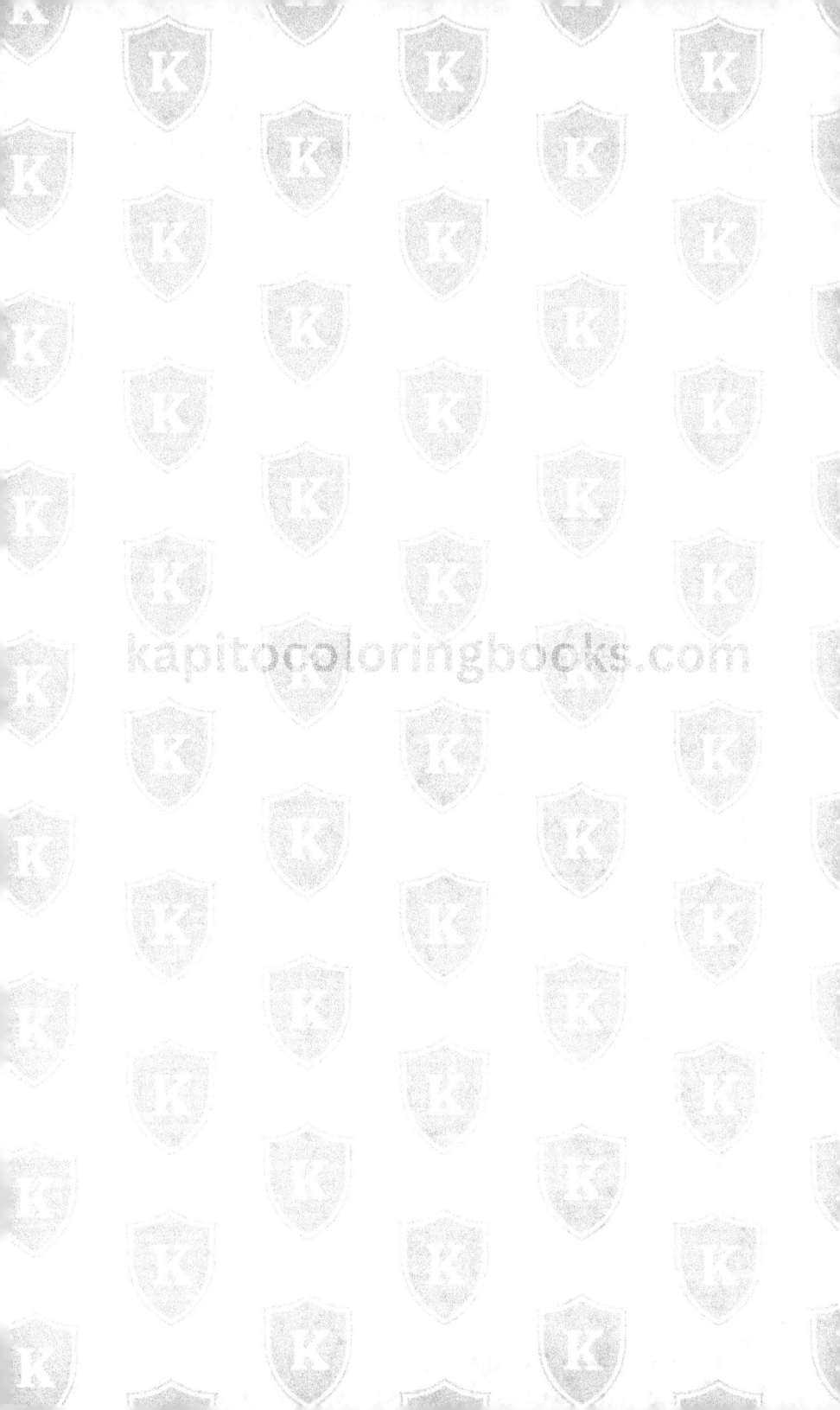

What's sadder than a hot air balloon without a beautiful landscape below it? Please provide and color...

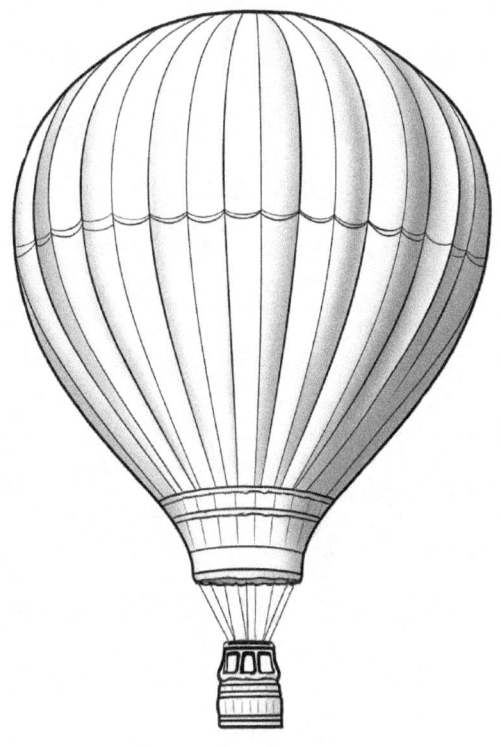

Did you pick a country or city landscape to draw? Maybe an ocean? Think about why...

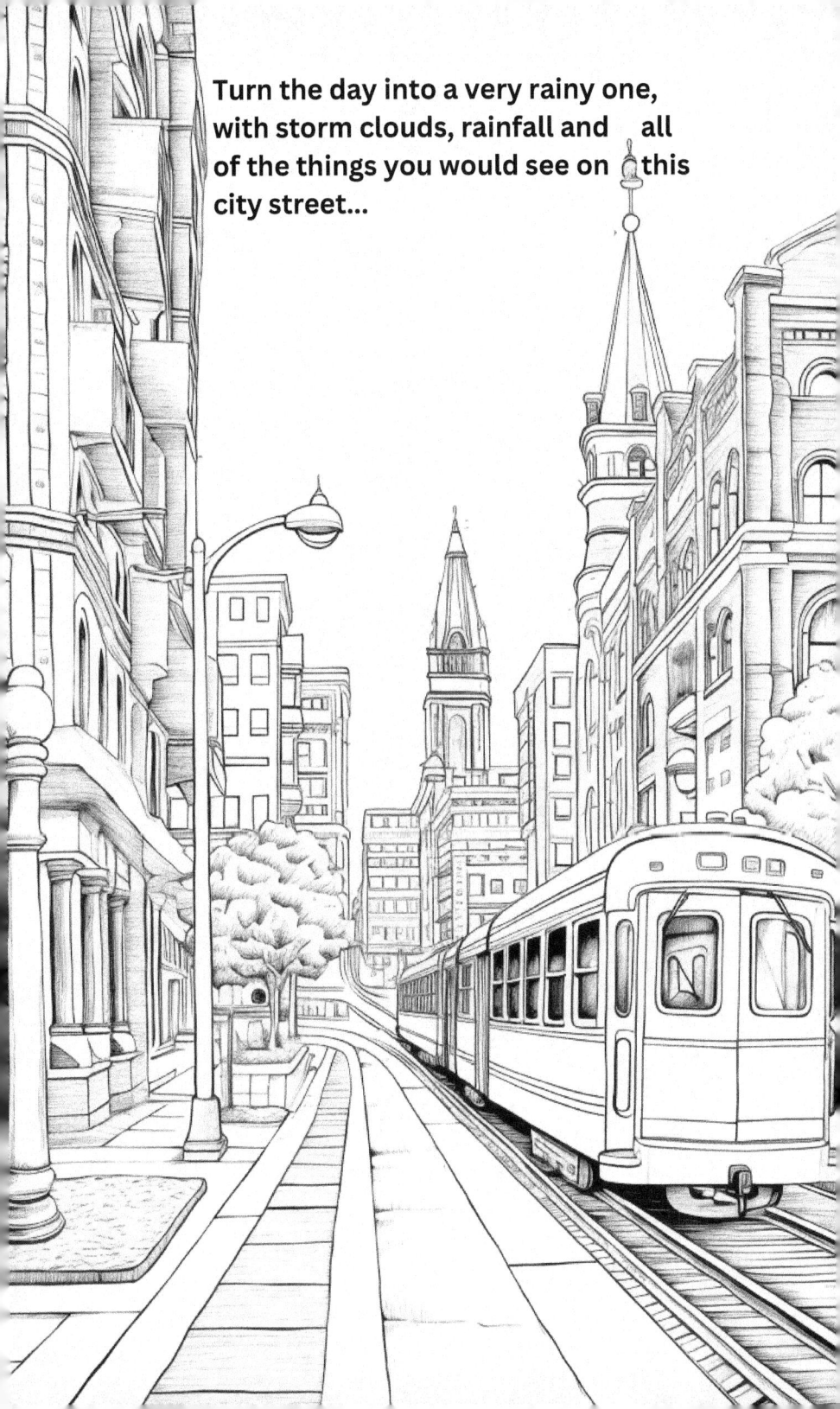

Turn the day into a very rainy one, with storm clouds, rainfall and all of the things you would see on this city street...

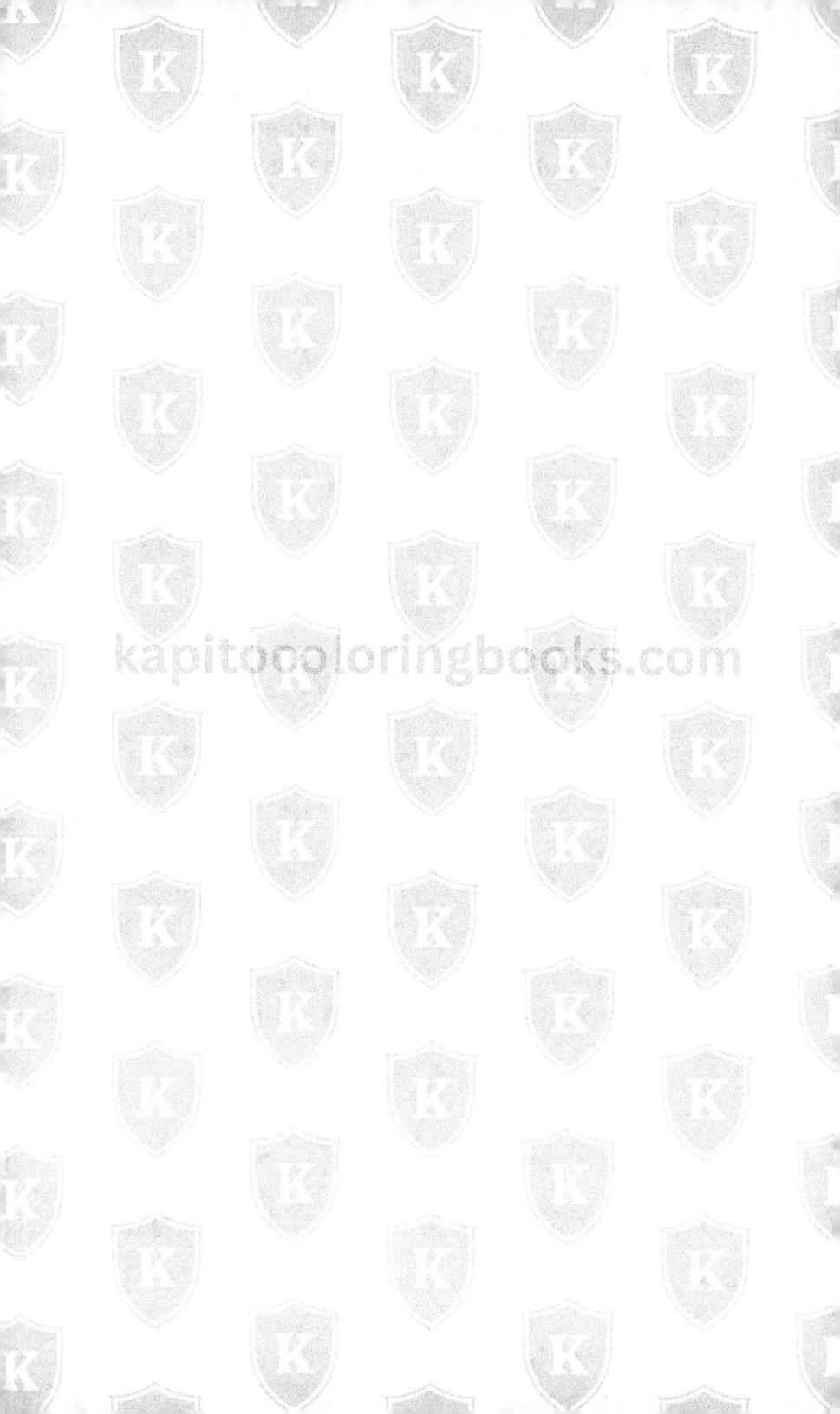

Did you know that there were supposed to be some houses on the left side of this path? Please draw in a row of homes, grass, etc., and then decorate and color!

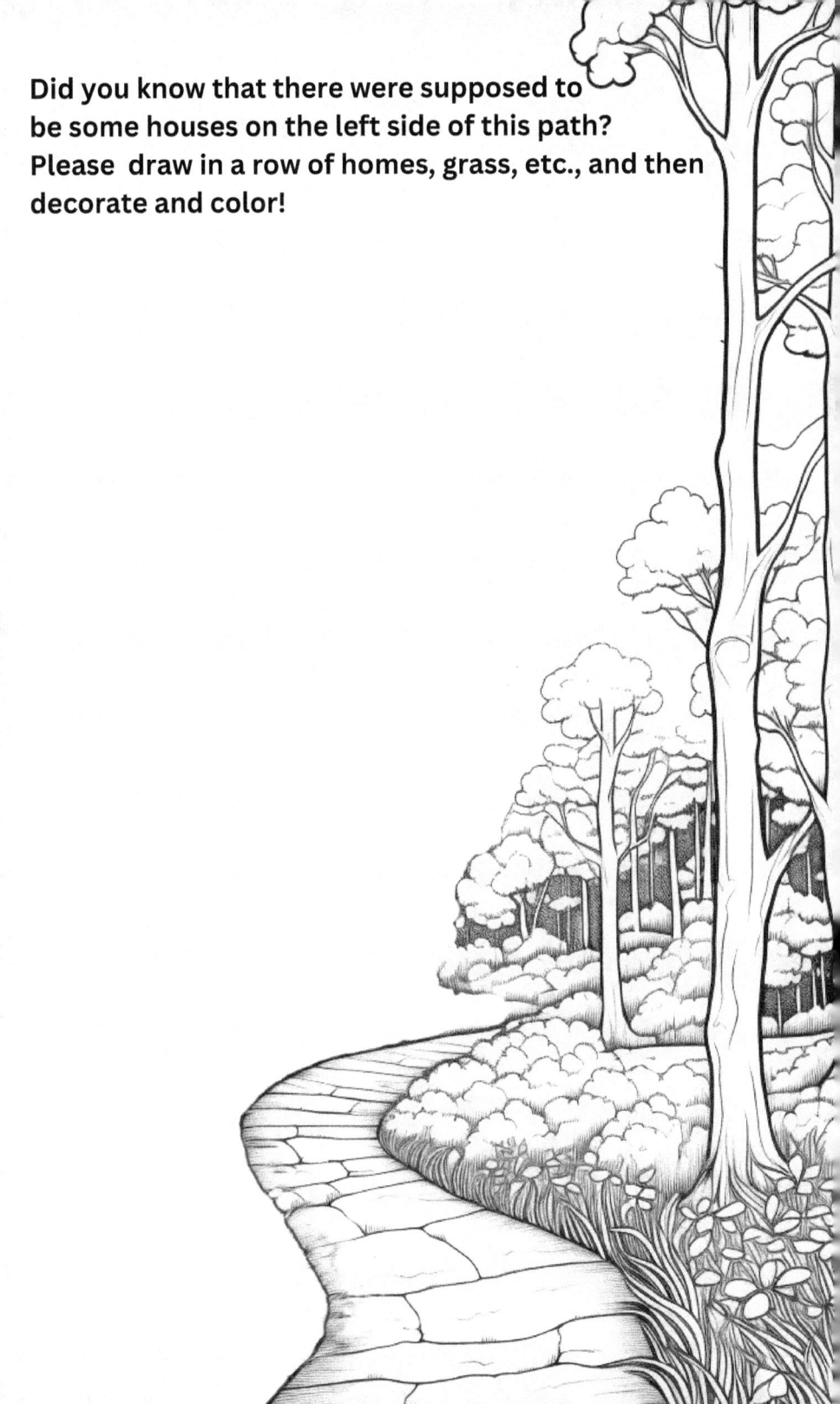

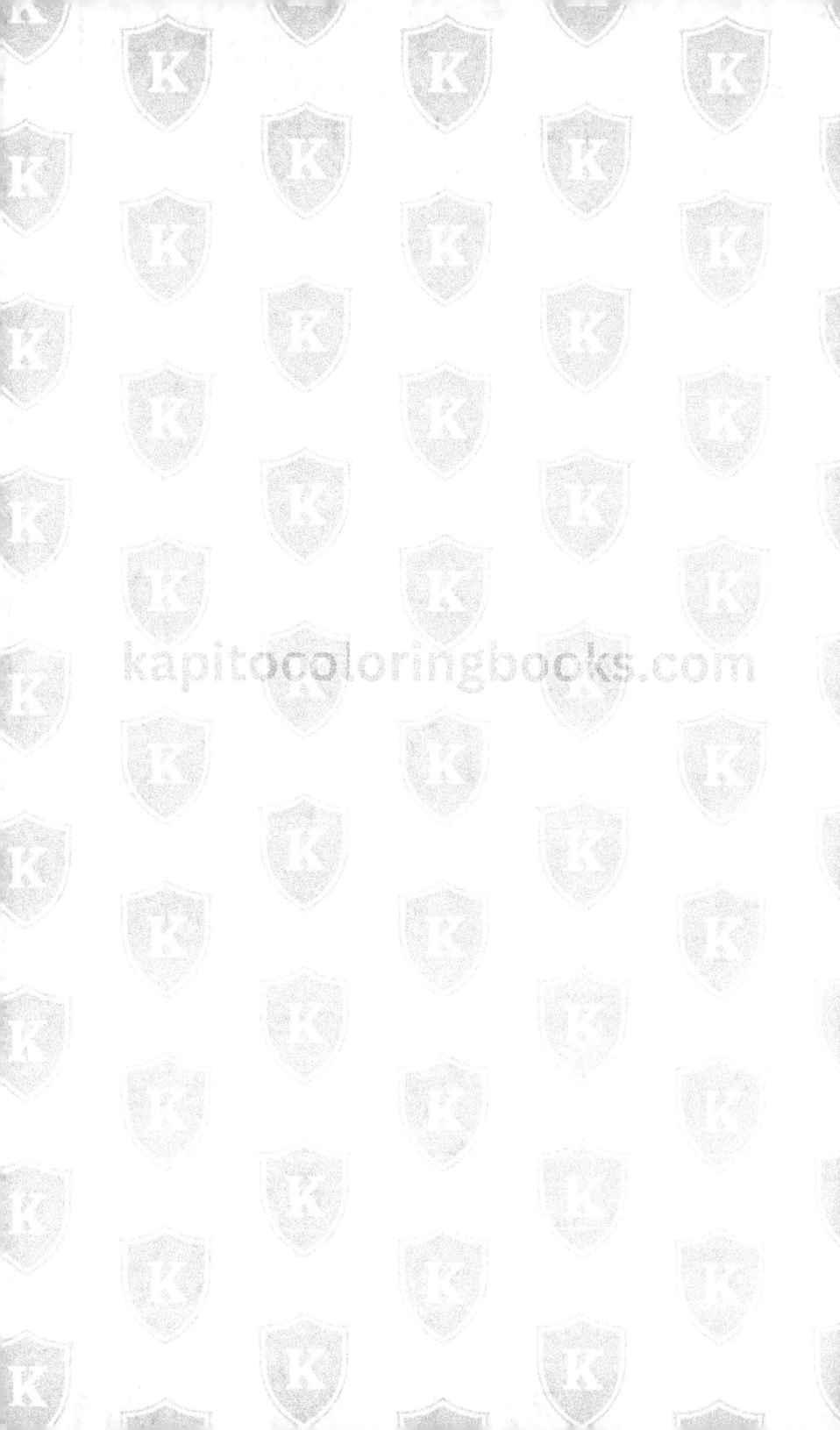

This is a sailboat, in need of a lake. And all of the things that come with a lake (trees, shorelines, clouds, etc...)

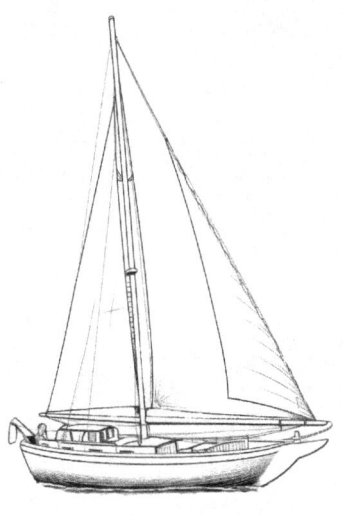

Just color. That's all. Then go for a walk.

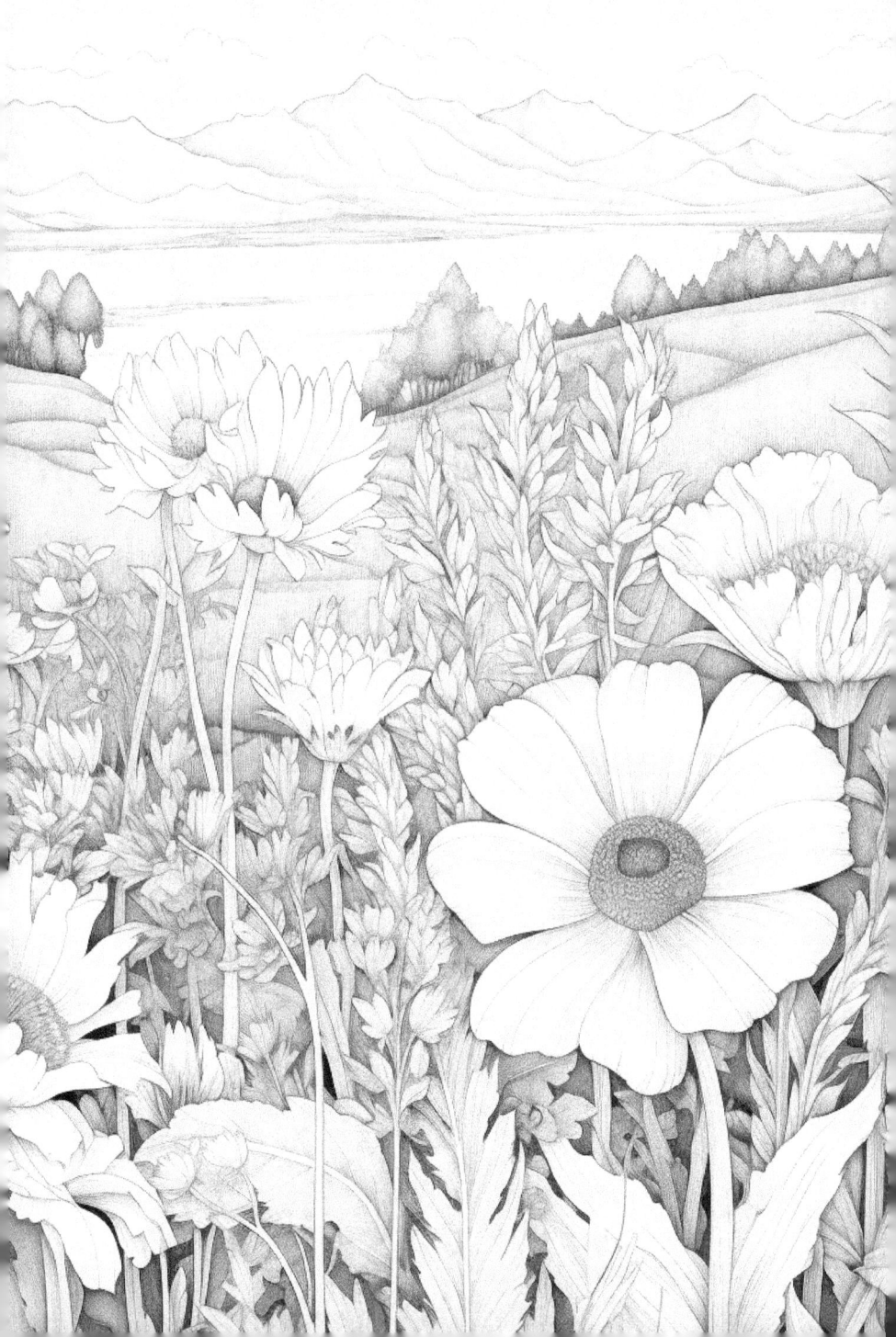

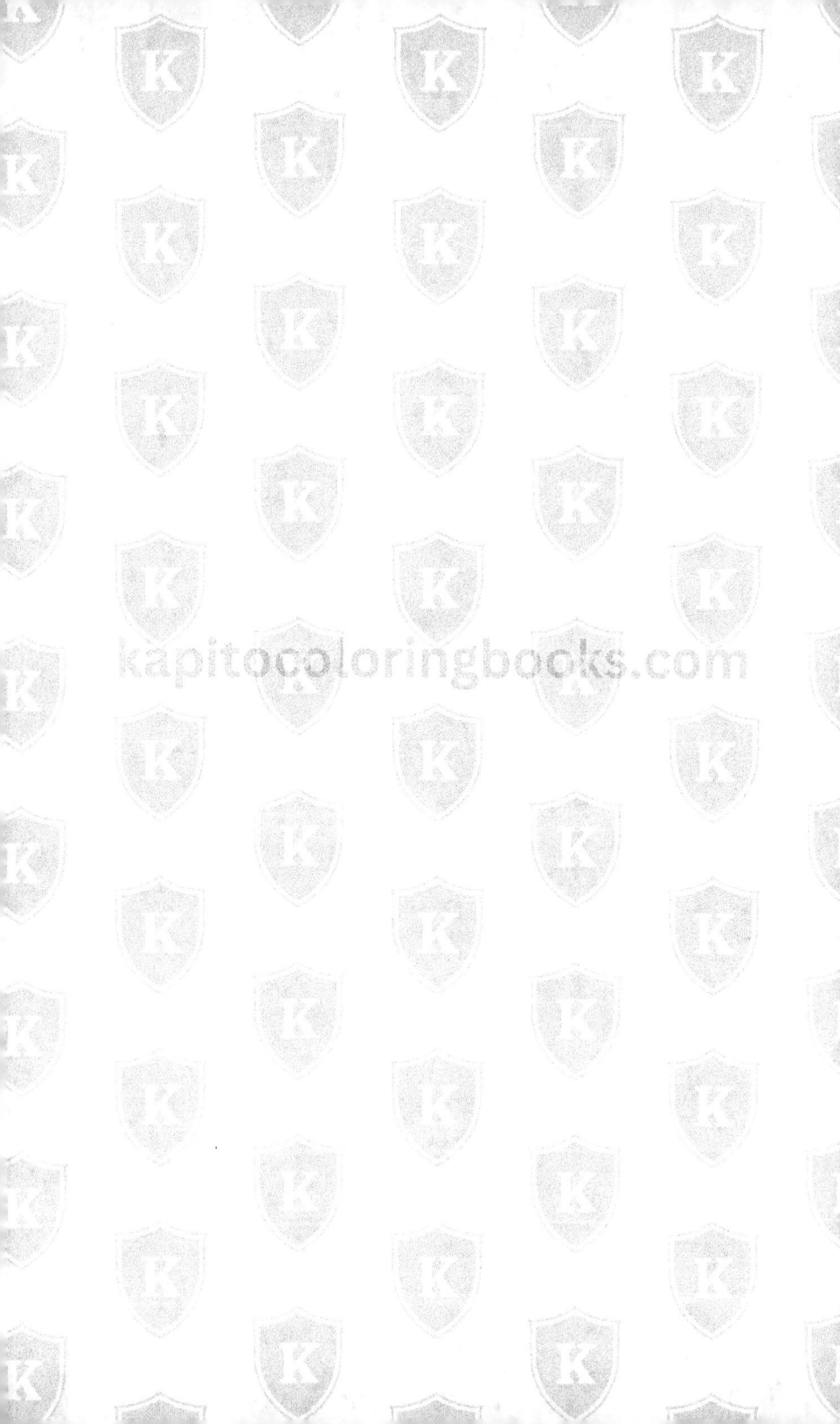

This poor guy is in need of a tropical island. Please draw him a very tall one with pretty trees.

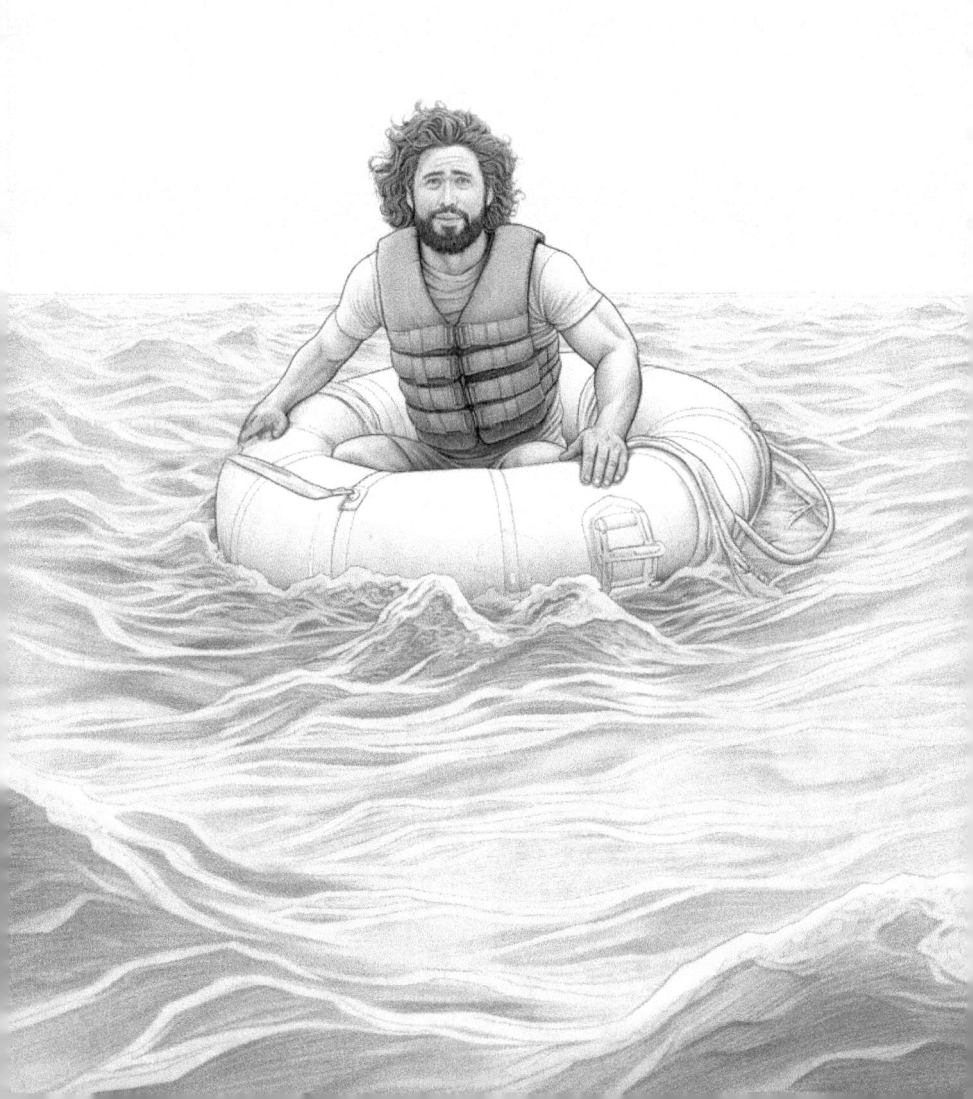

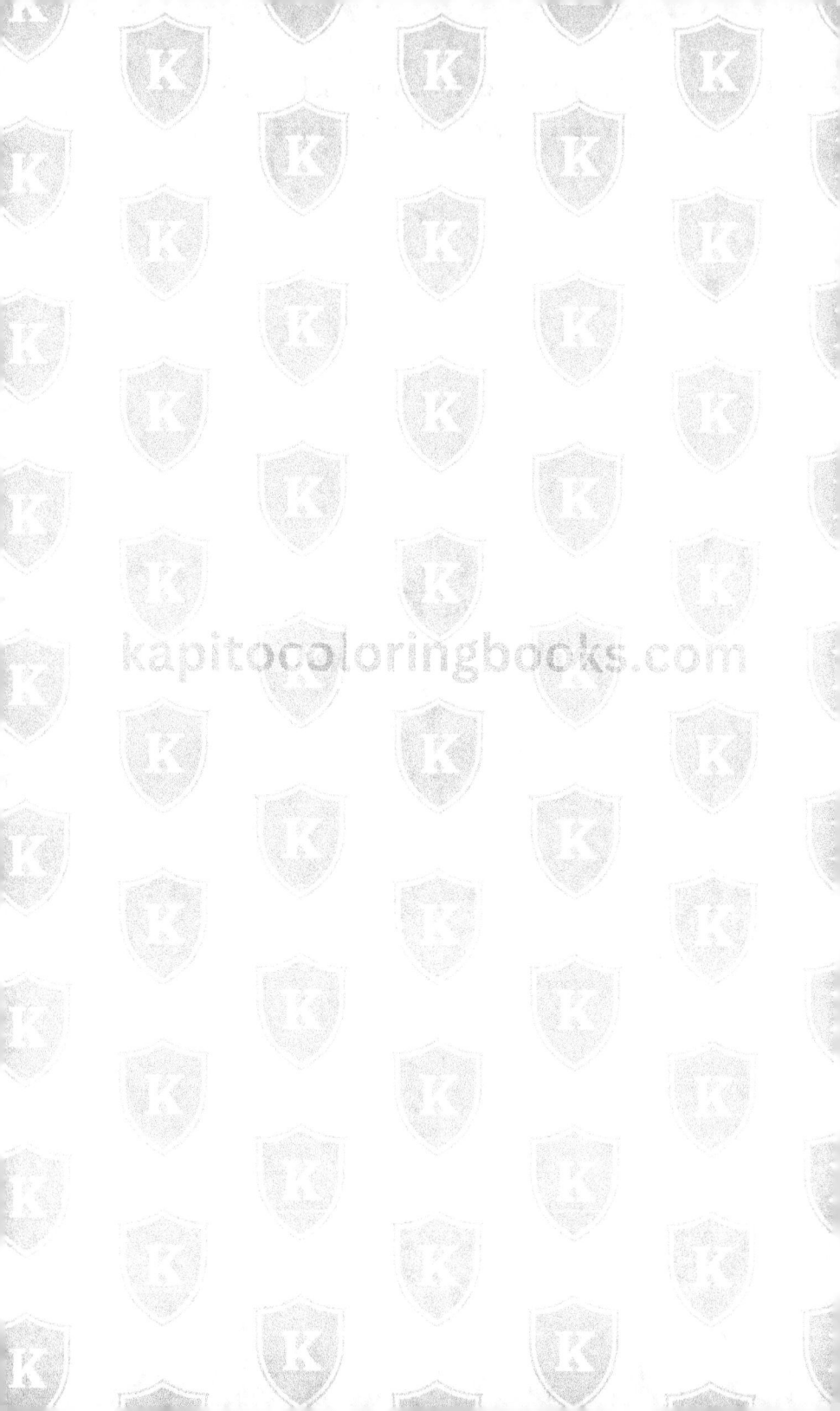

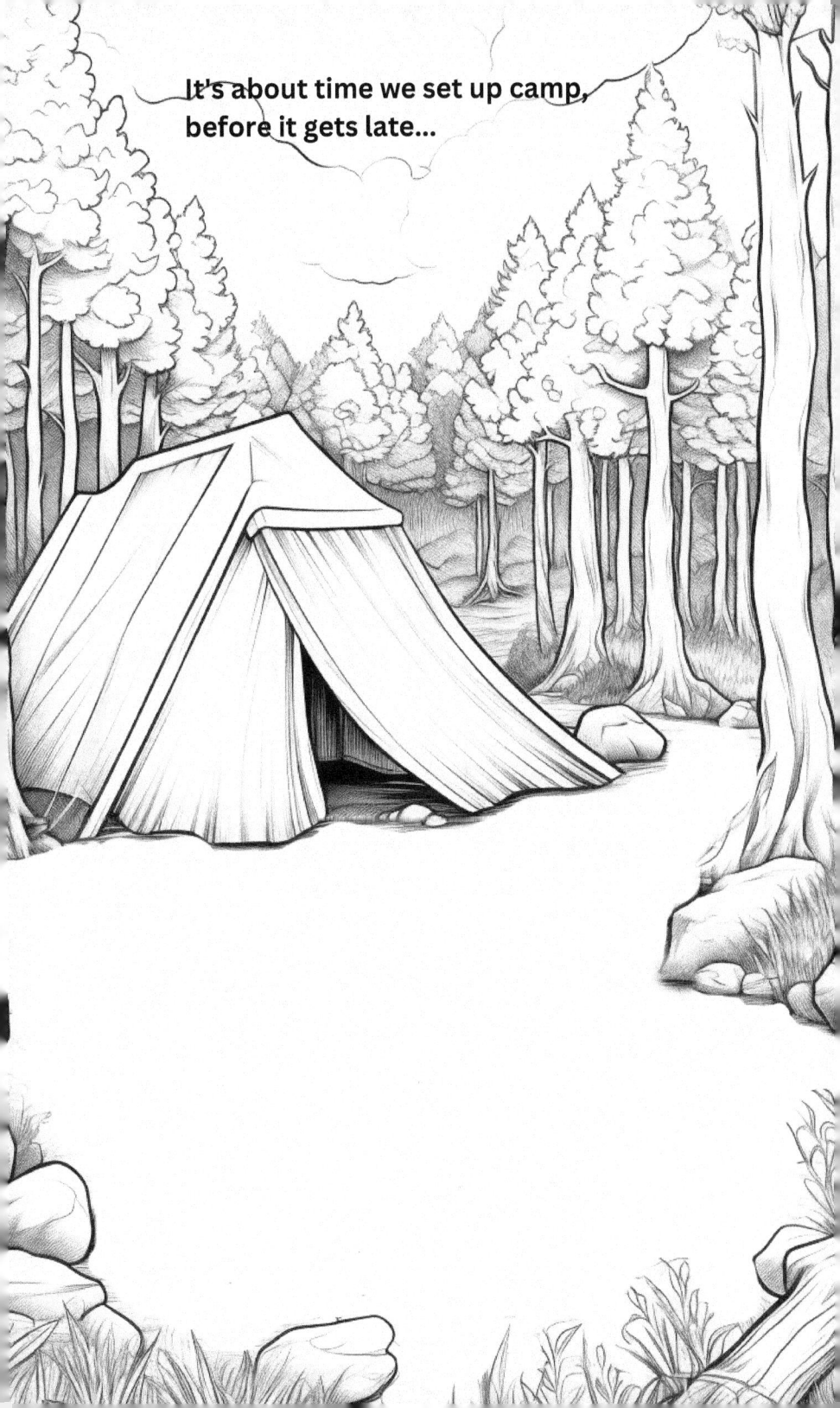

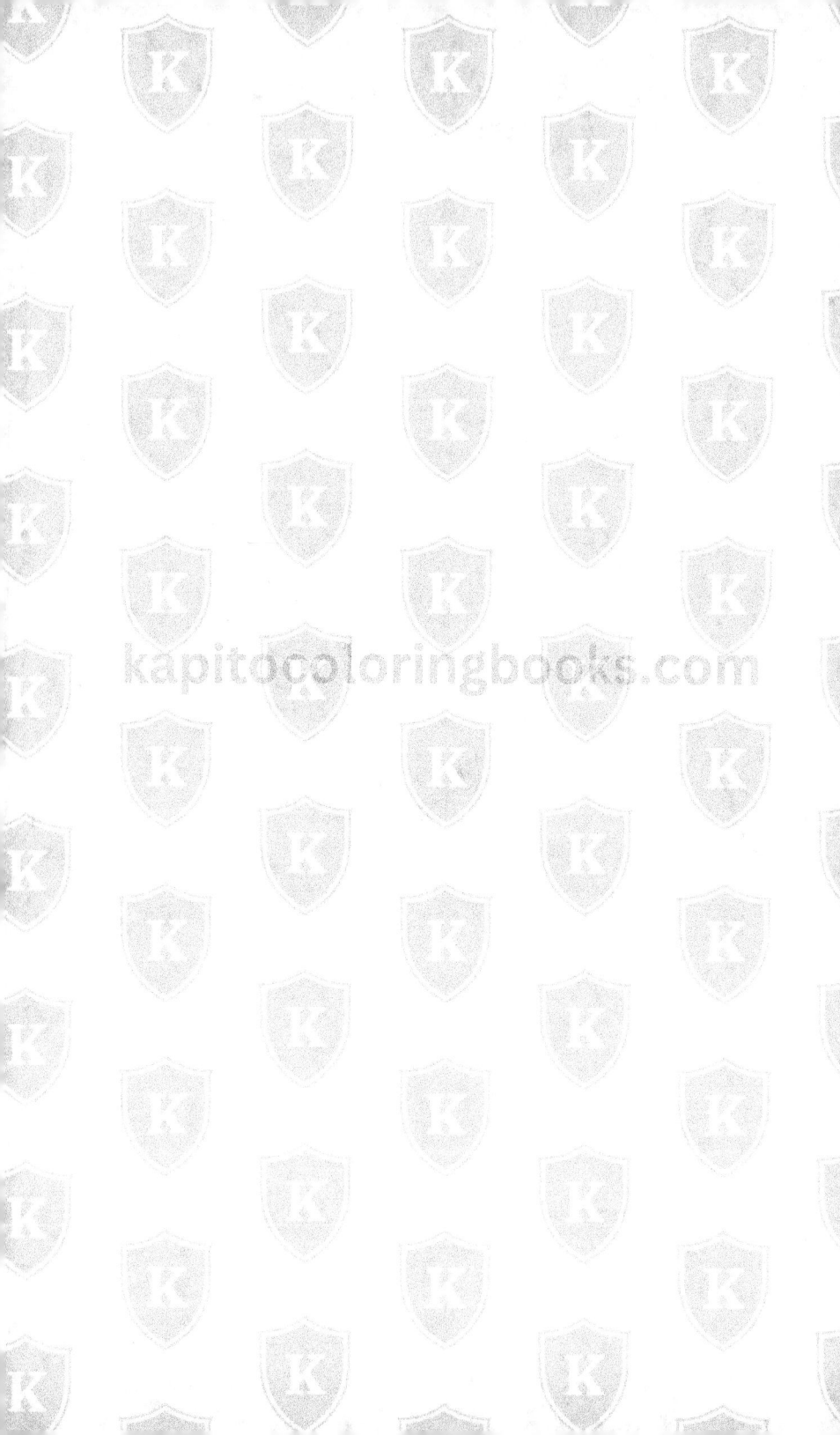

This backyard bbq lunch seems to be missing a backyard. Please draw one in and color as you please.

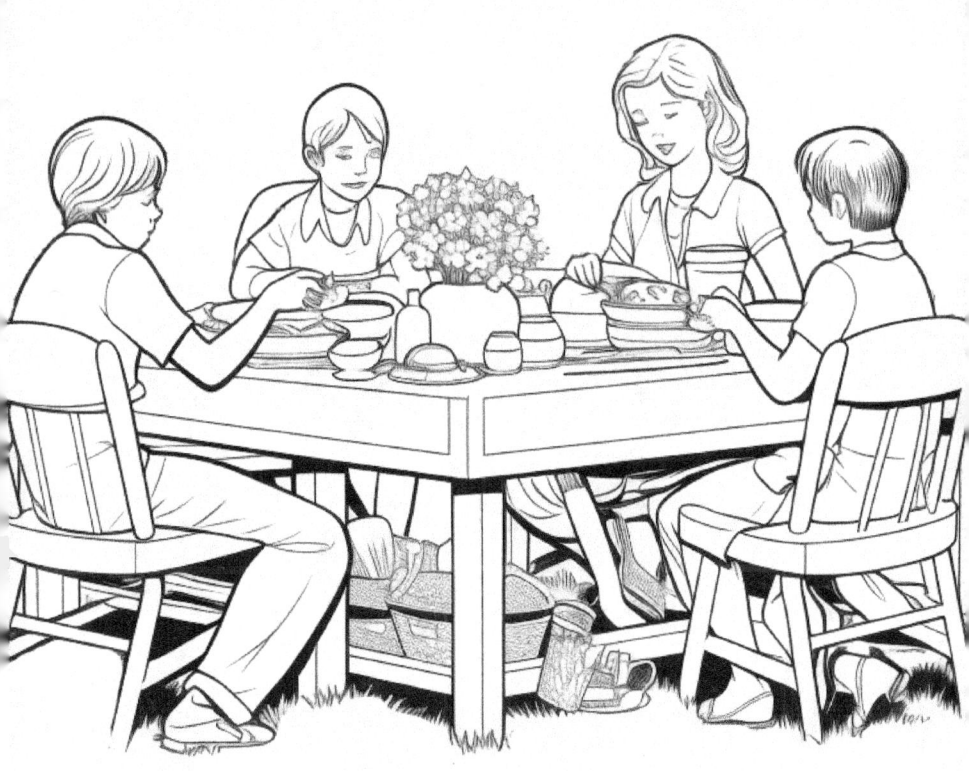

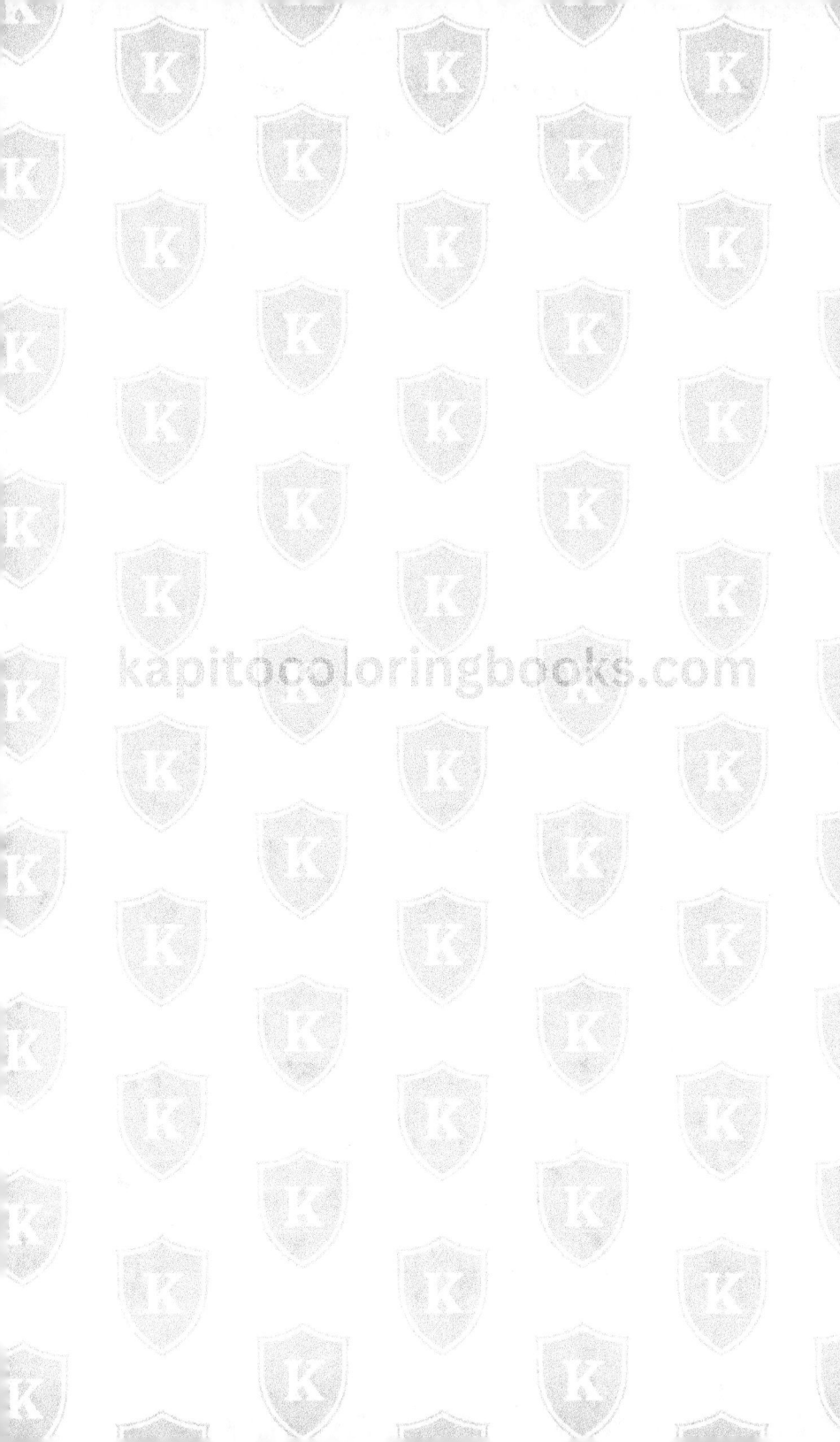

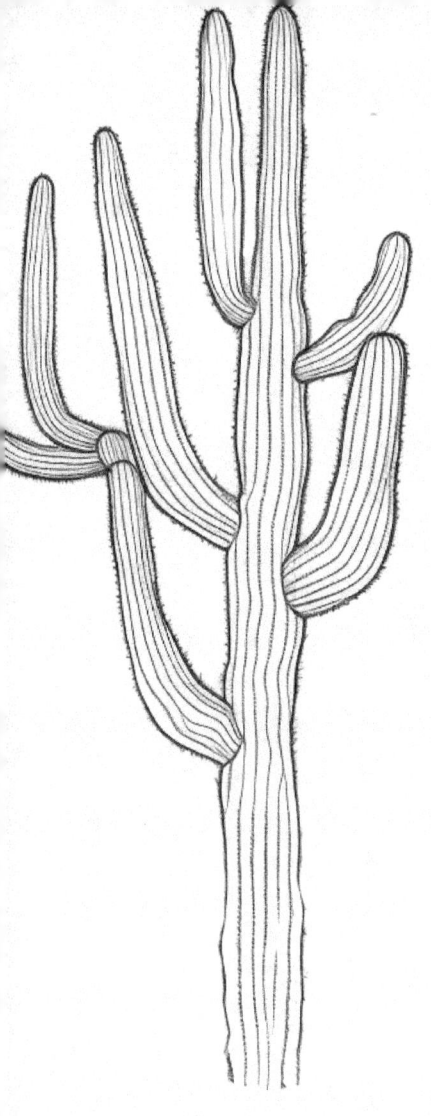

It's time for a desert landscape. We started with a cactus. And a rock. So the hard part's over, right?

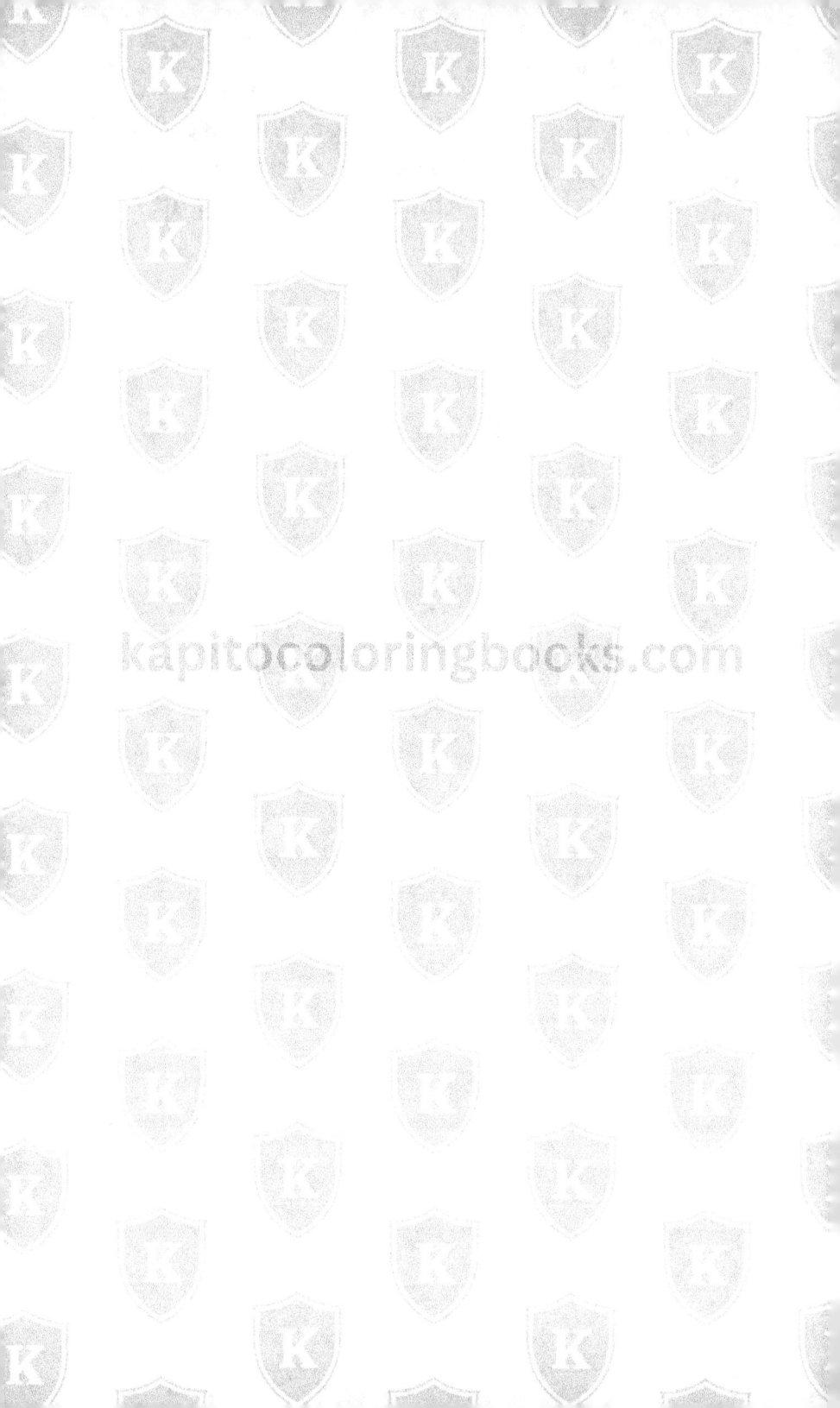

These lovely and peaceful waterfalls are in need of a majestic mountain backdrop. Are you up for the task?

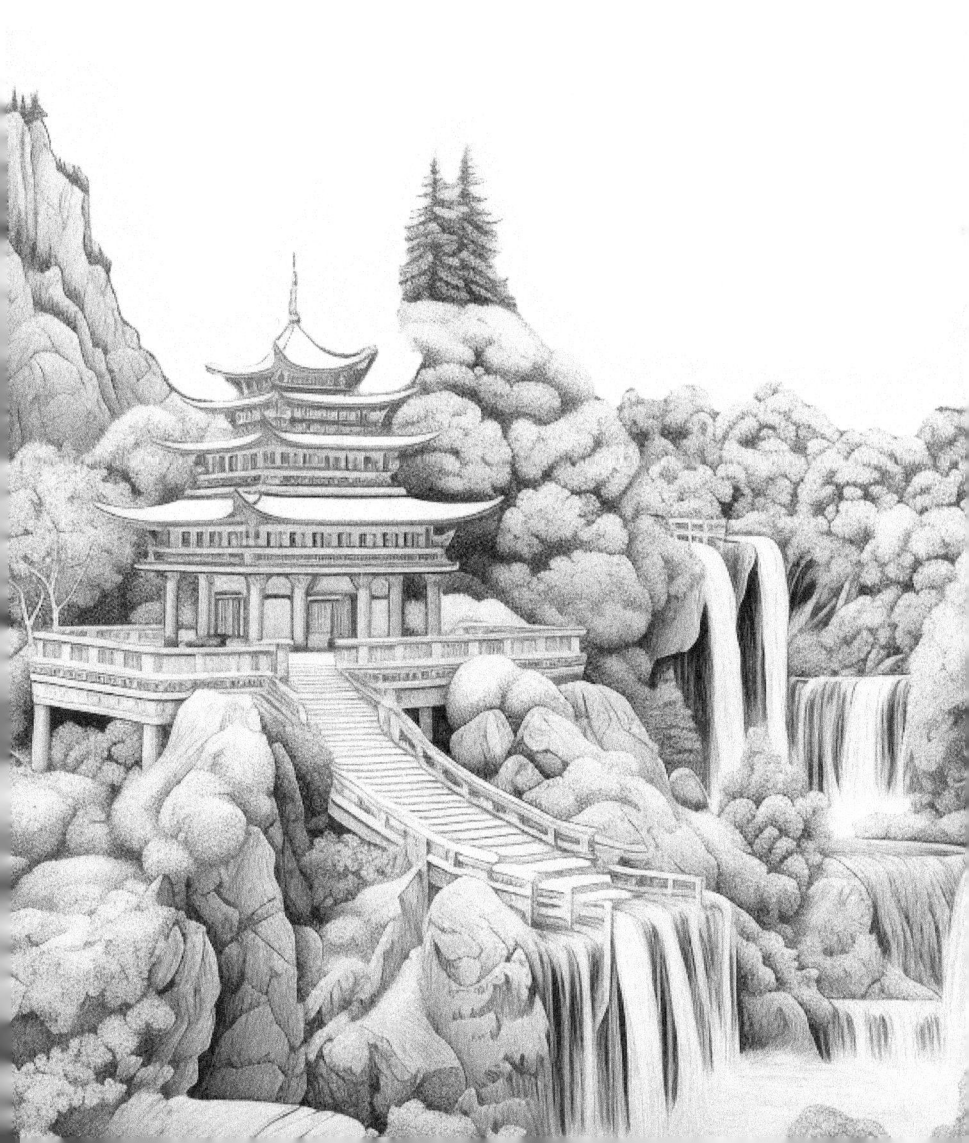

Pretty cool car, huh? Place it wherever you'd like with a cool backdrop. Get really creative!

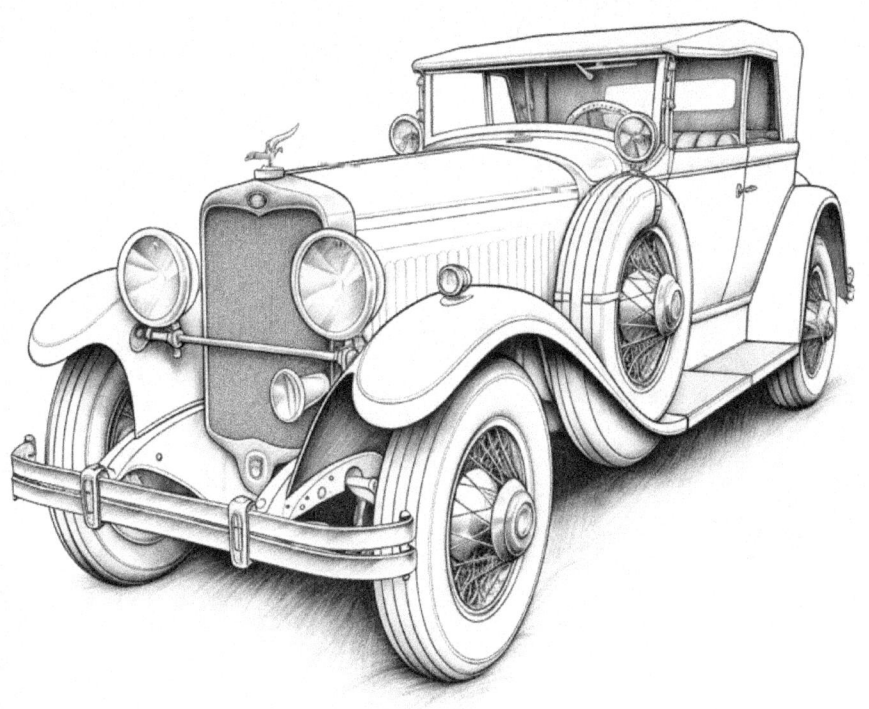

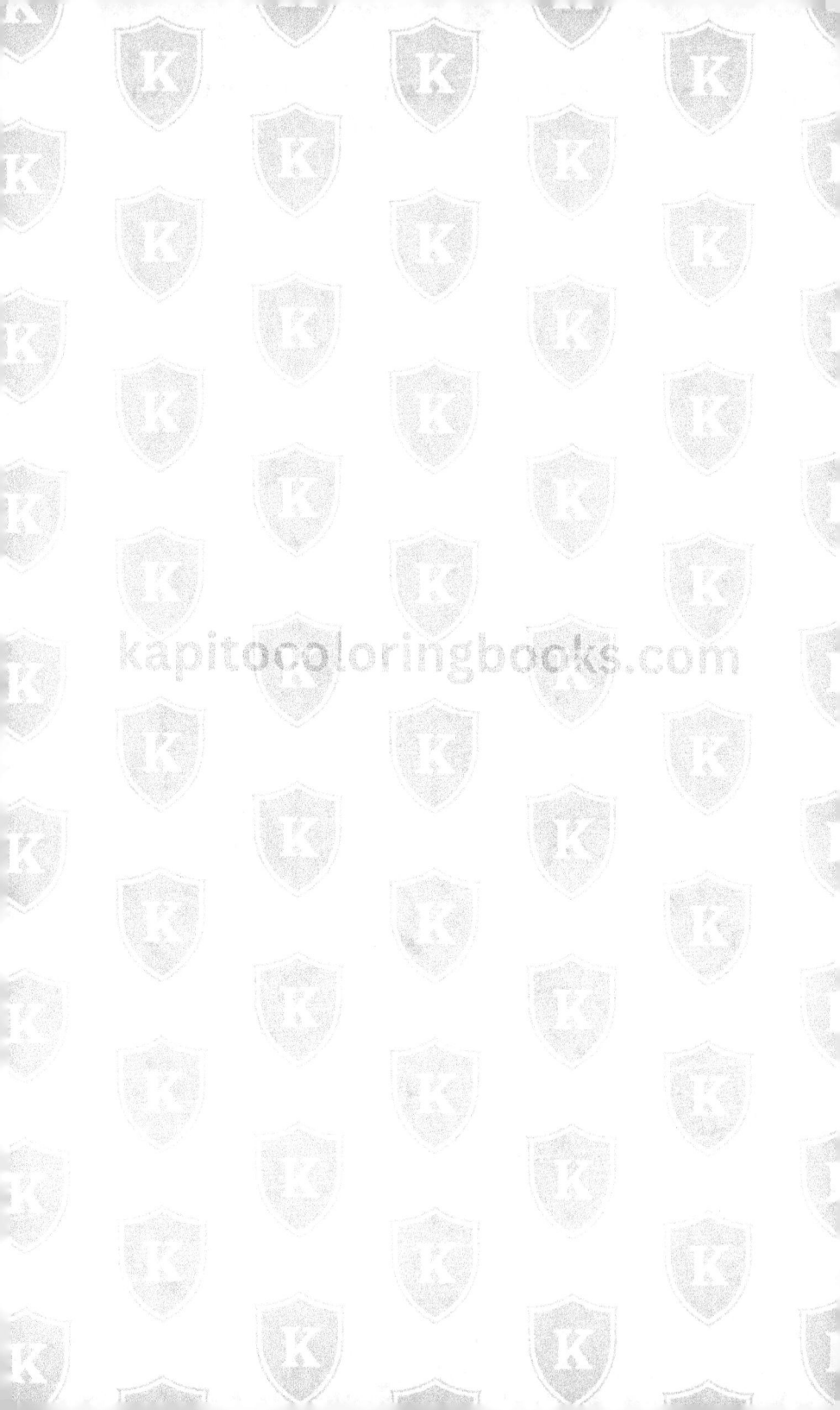

Time for a serene farm scene. We got you started with a windmill. This should be a breeze!

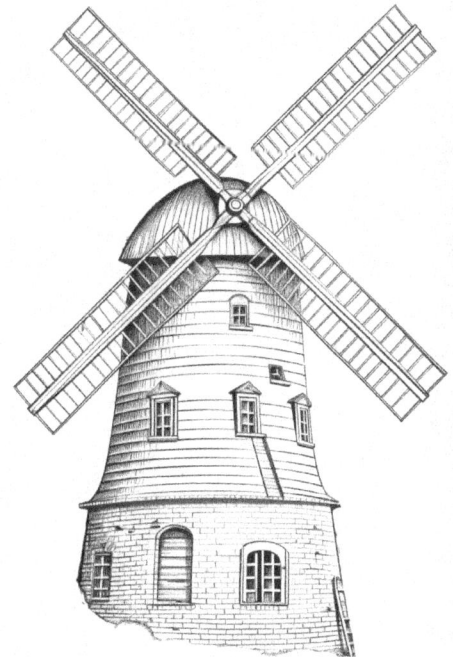

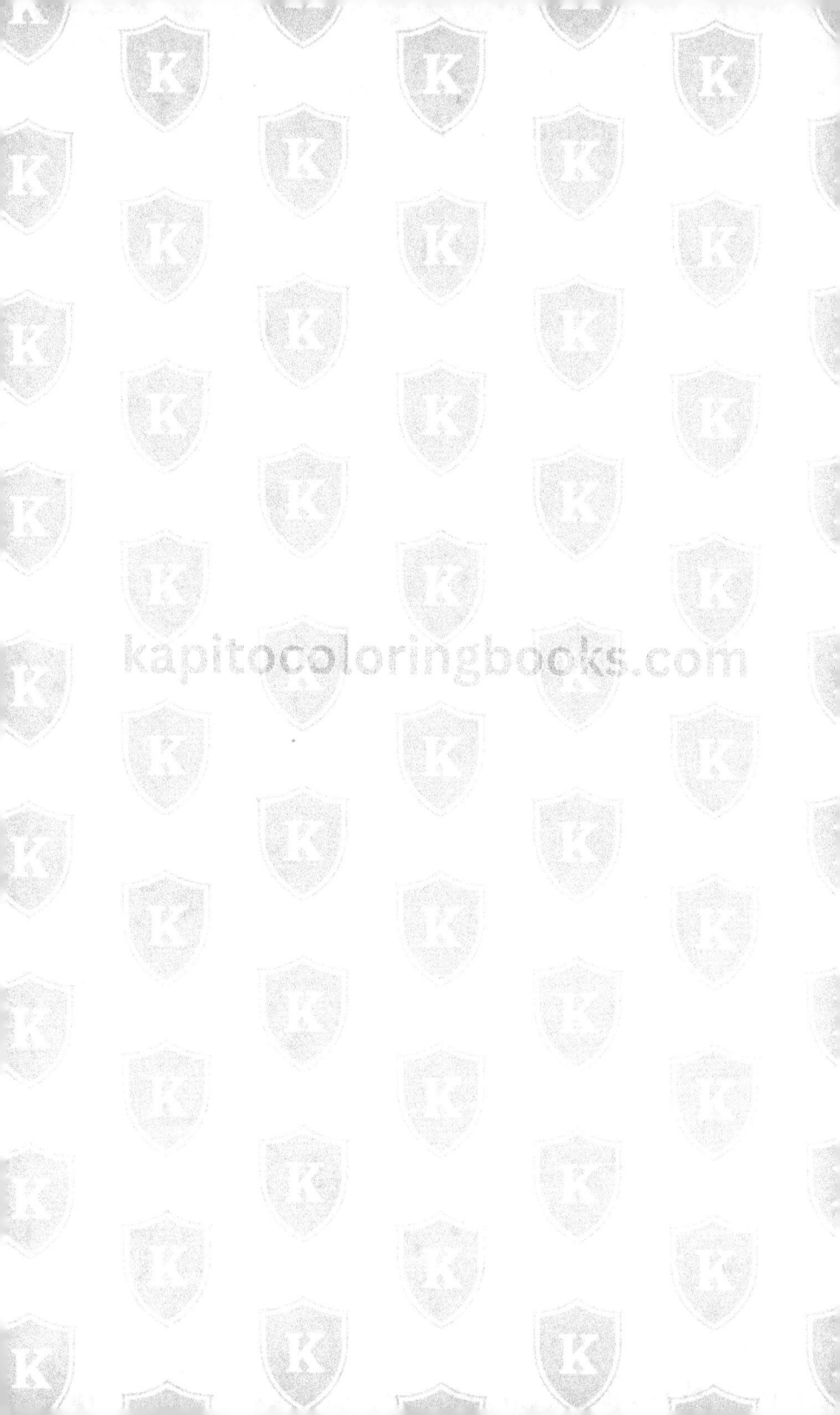

This apartment certainly has plenty of houseplants. How about decorating the rest of it?

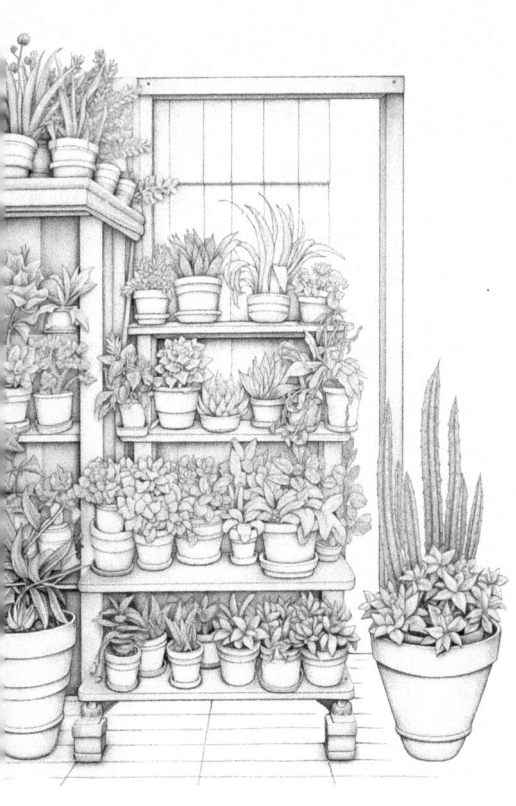

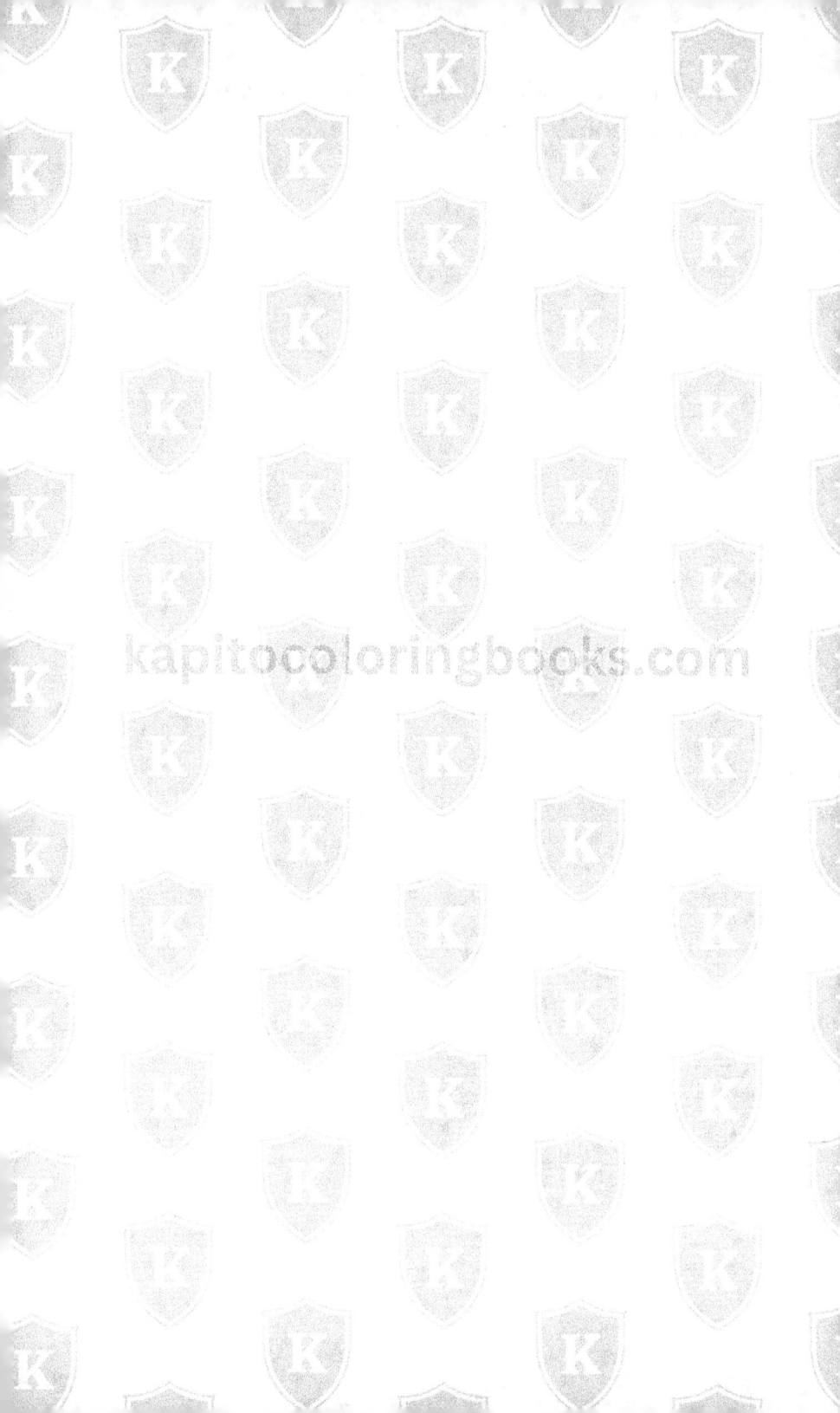

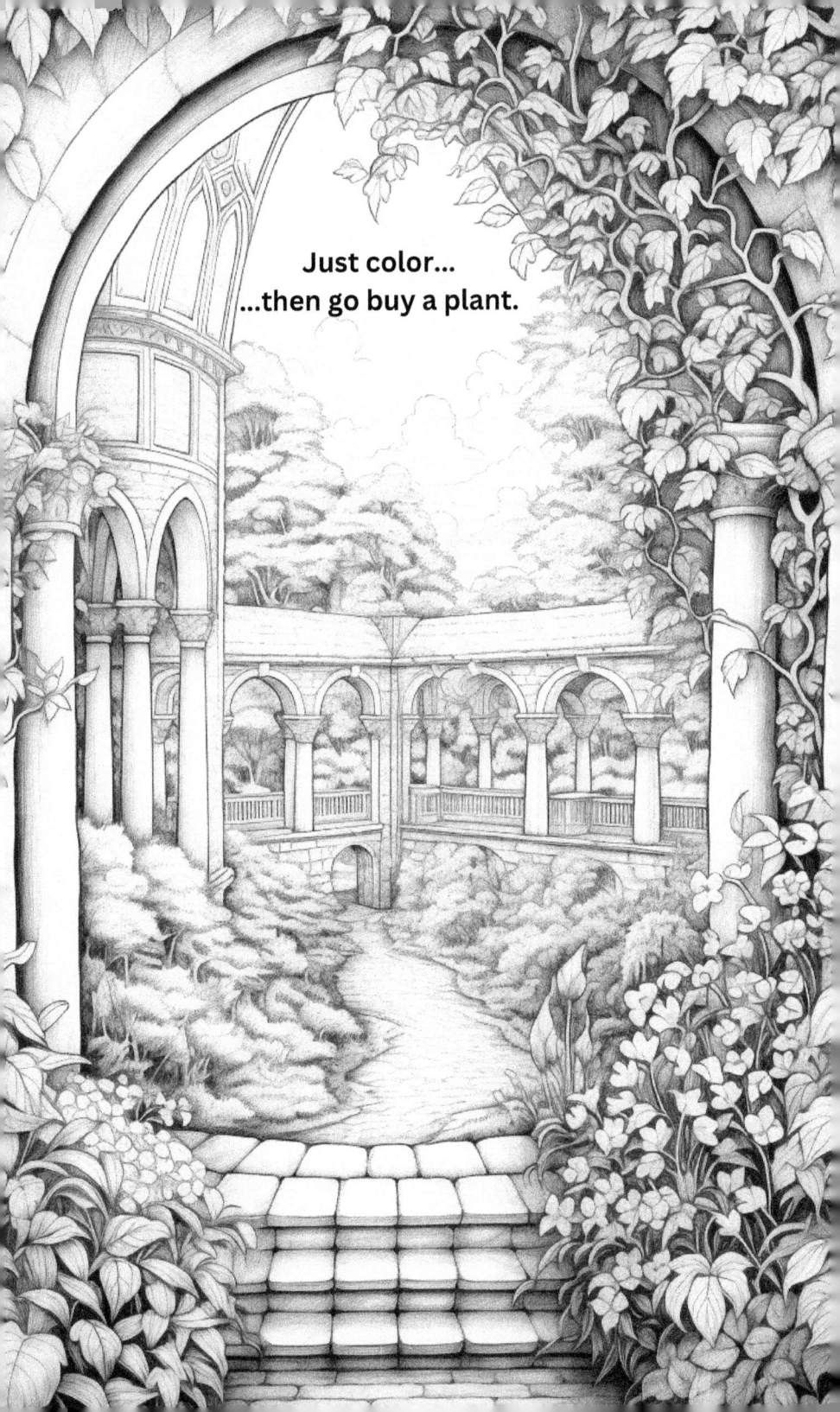

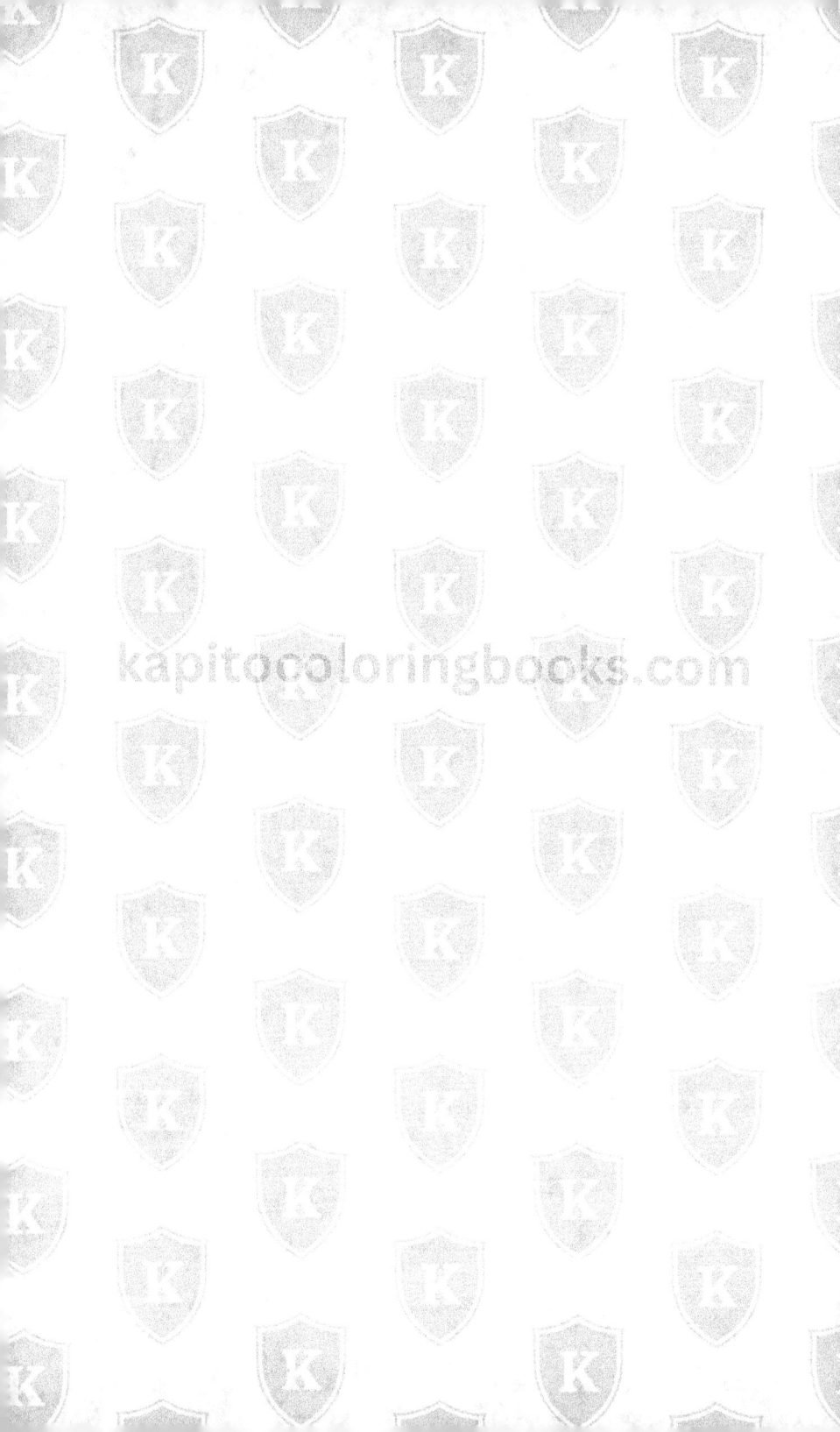

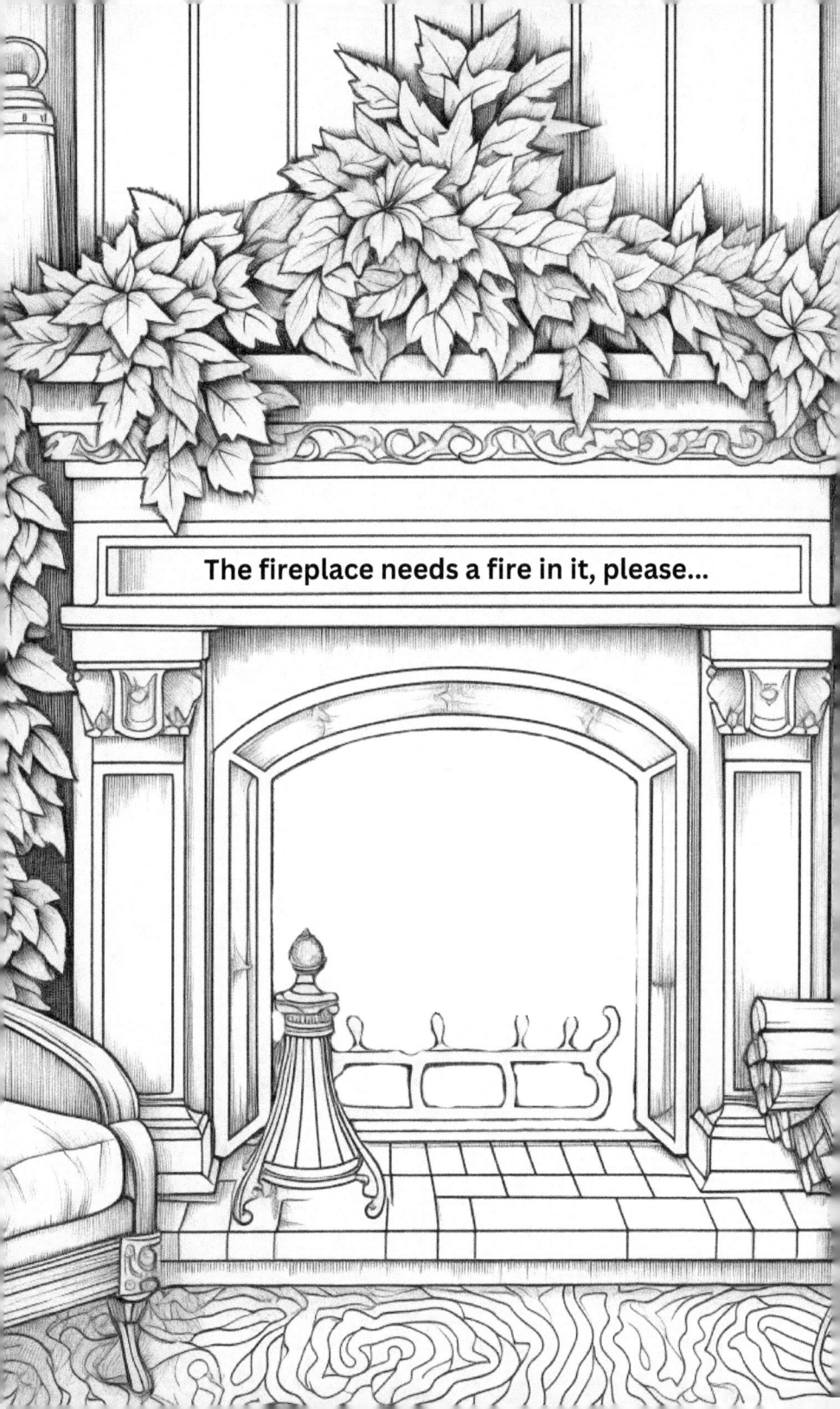

The fireplace needs a fire in it, please...

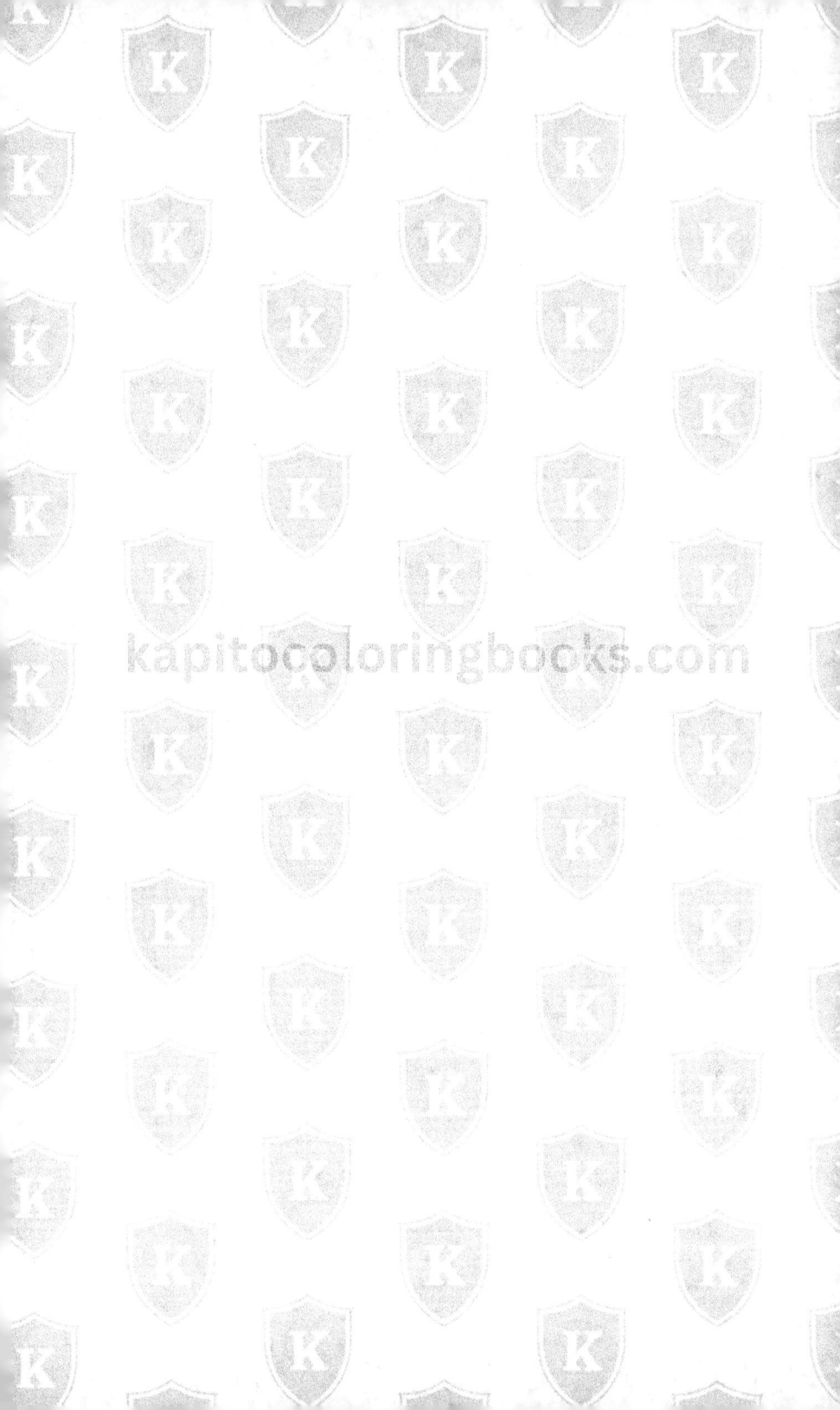

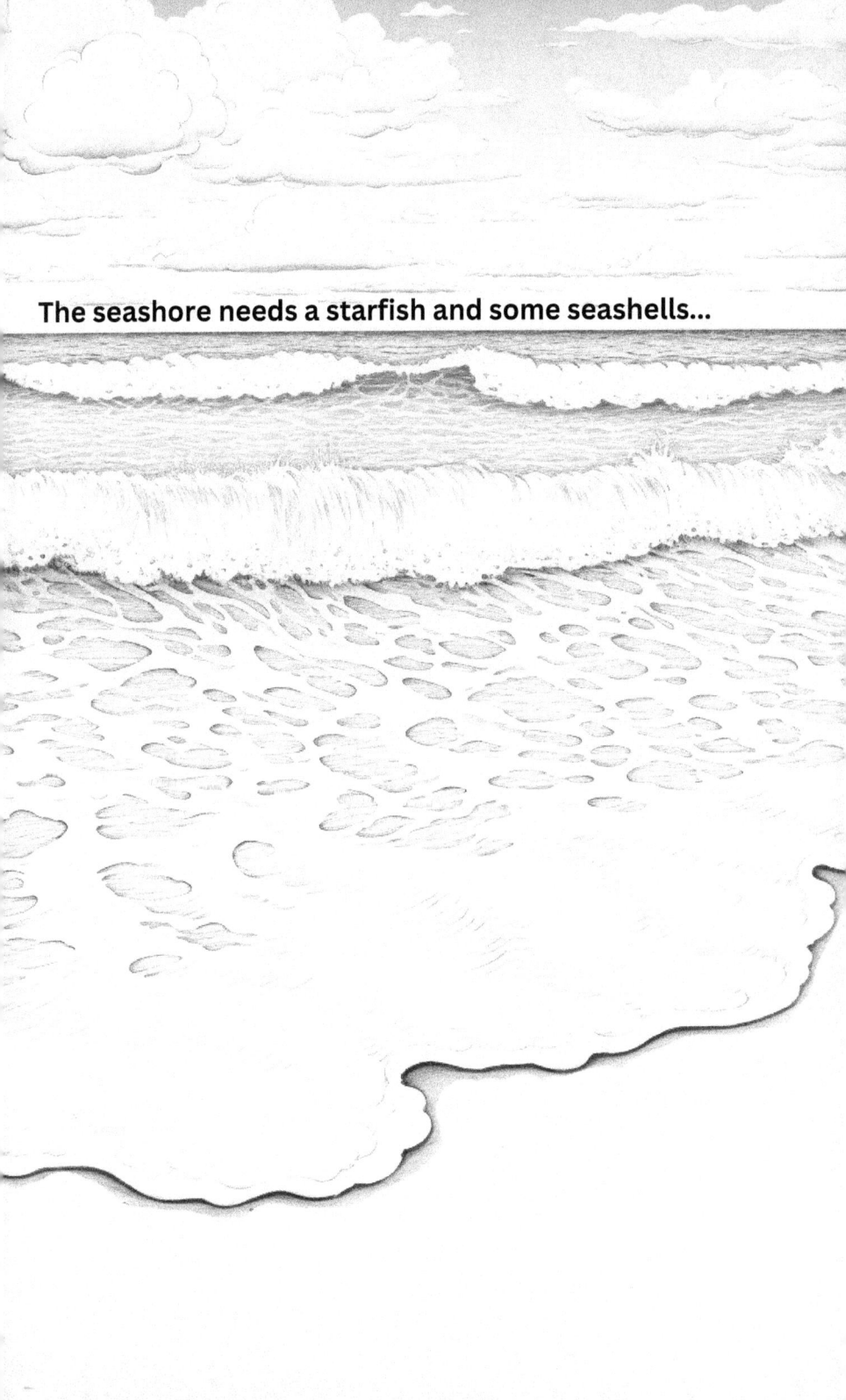

The seashore needs a starfish and some seashells...

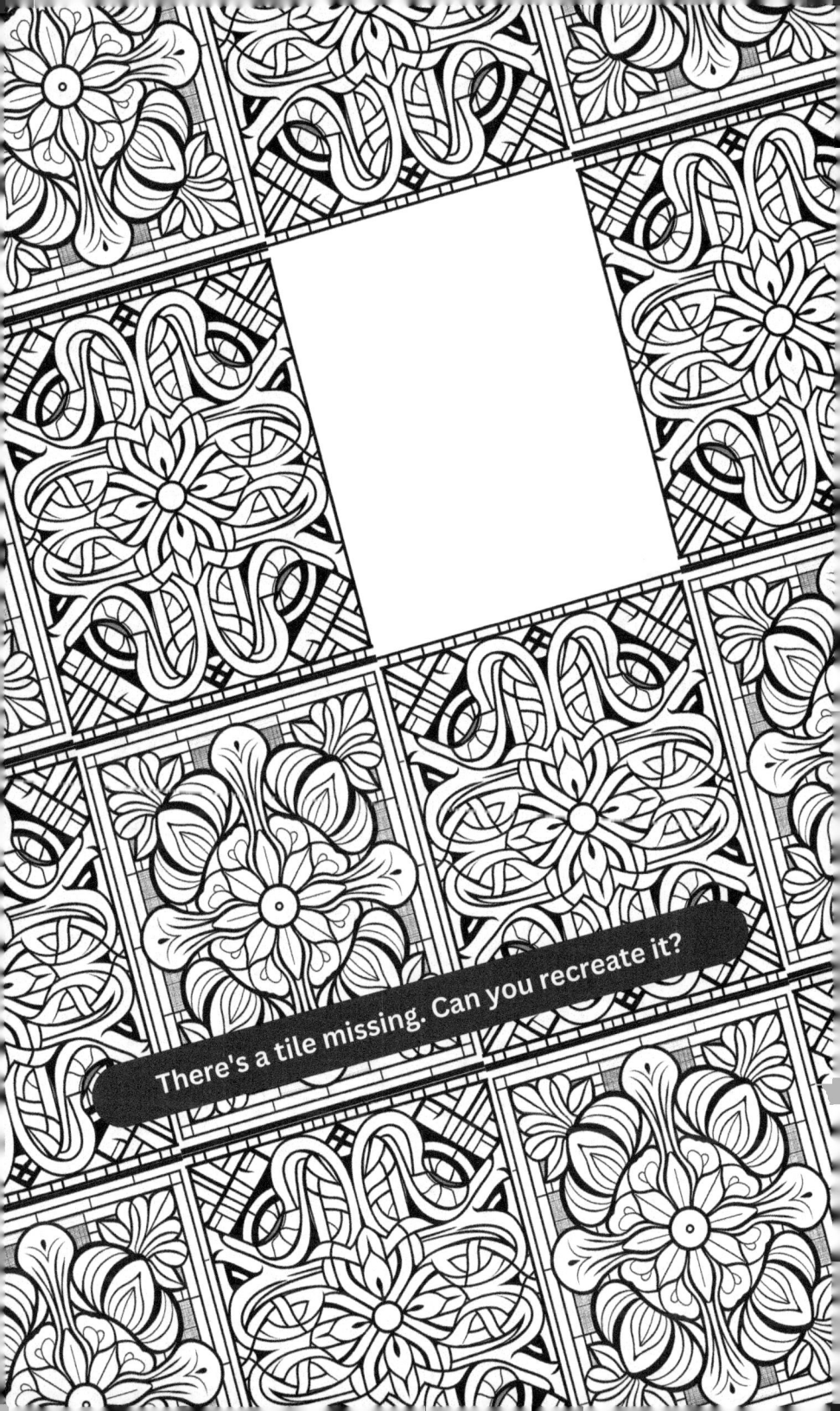

There's a tile missing. Can you recreate it?

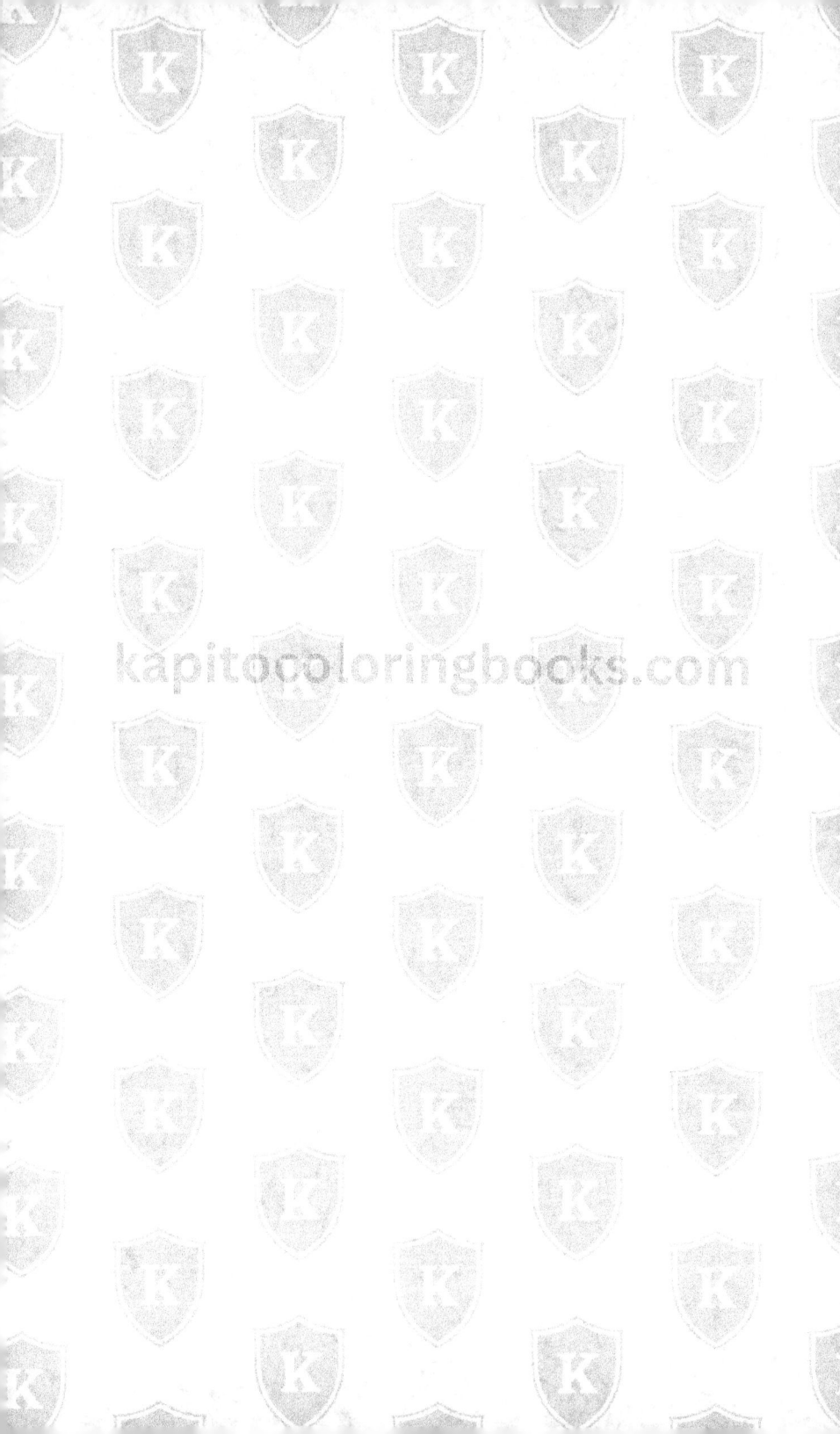

Where is this bridge coming from? Where is it going?

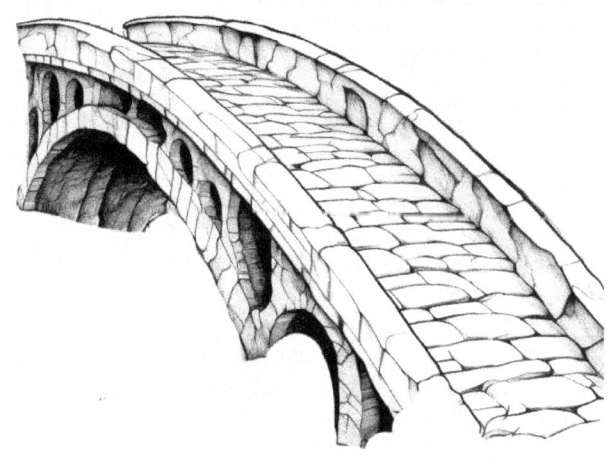

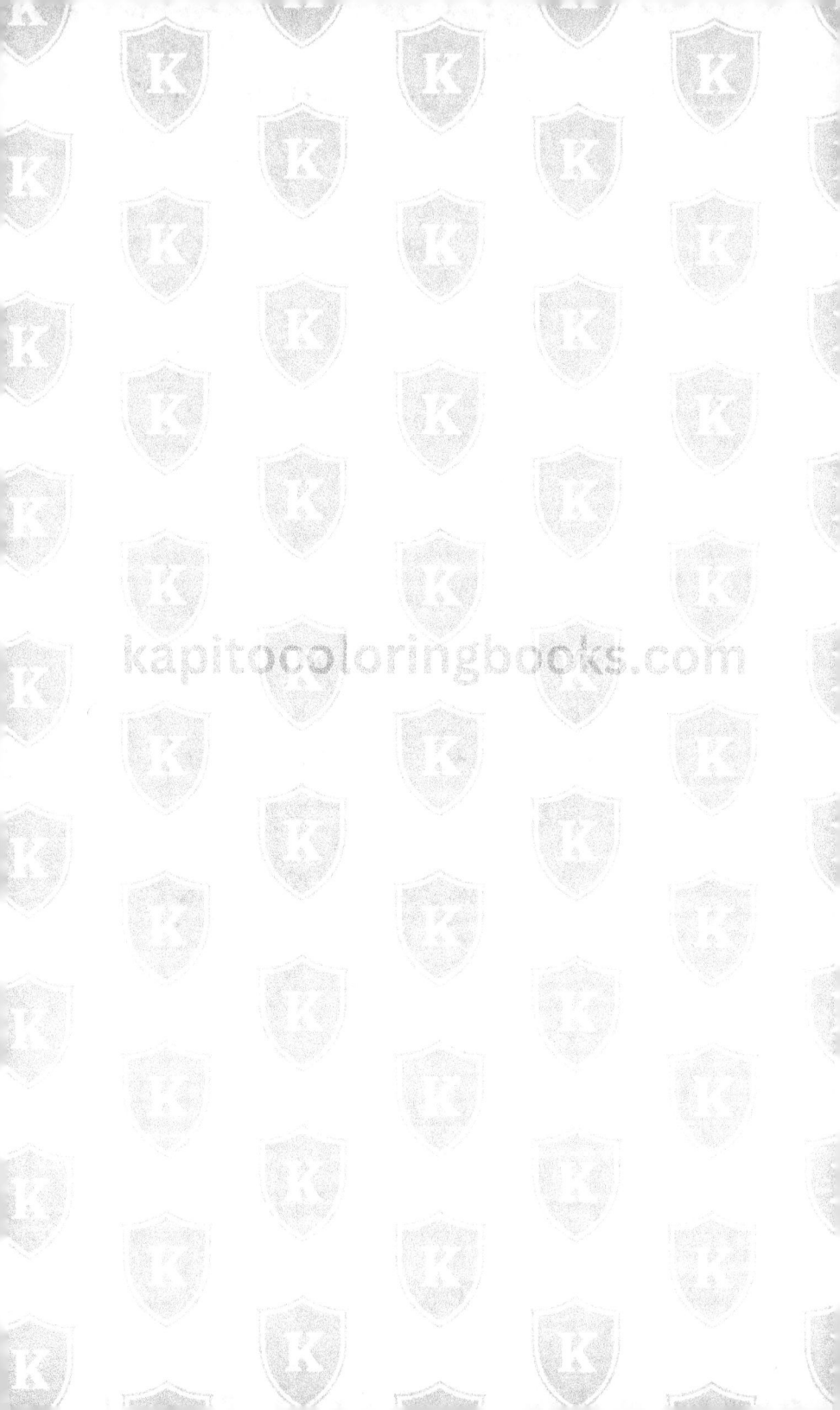

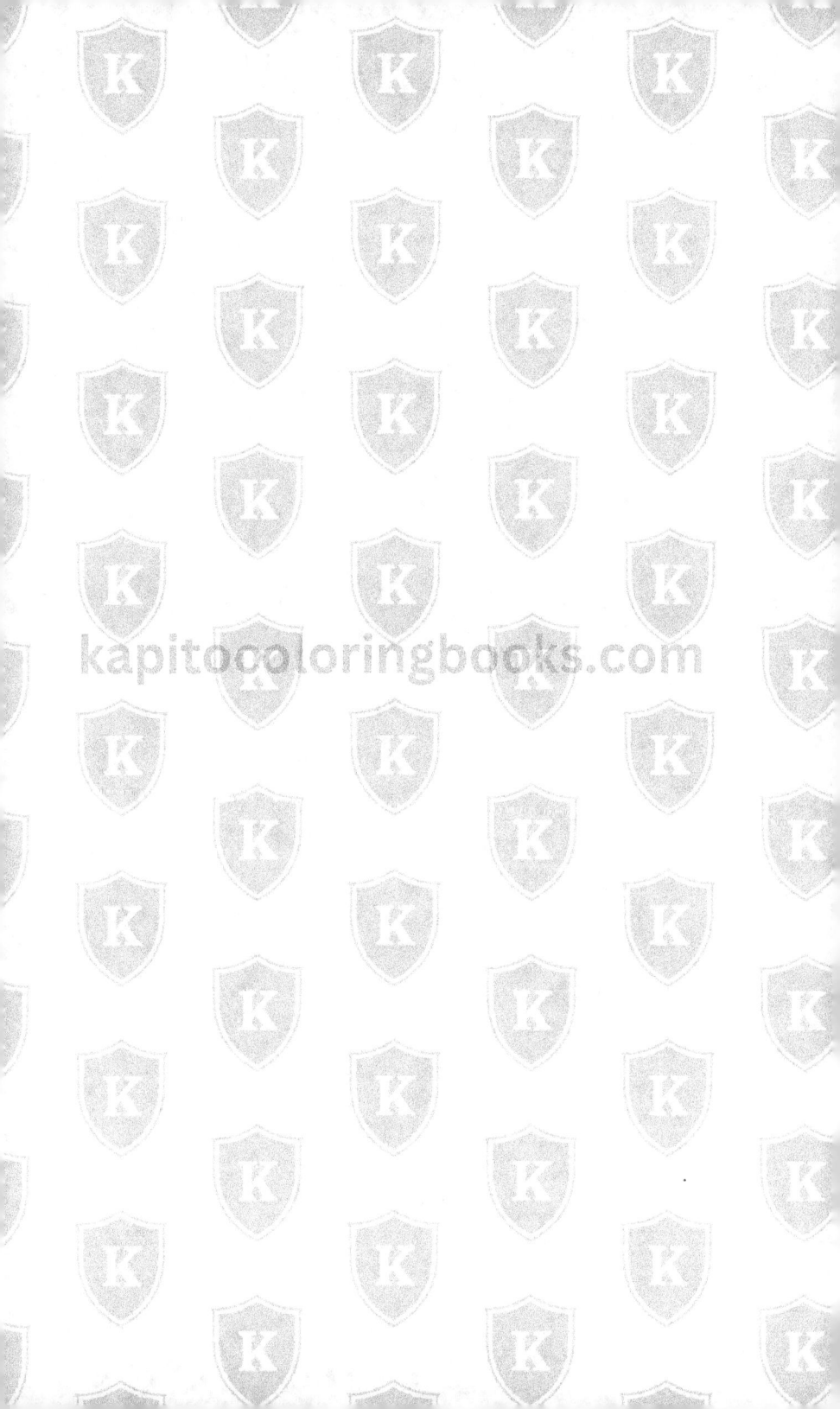

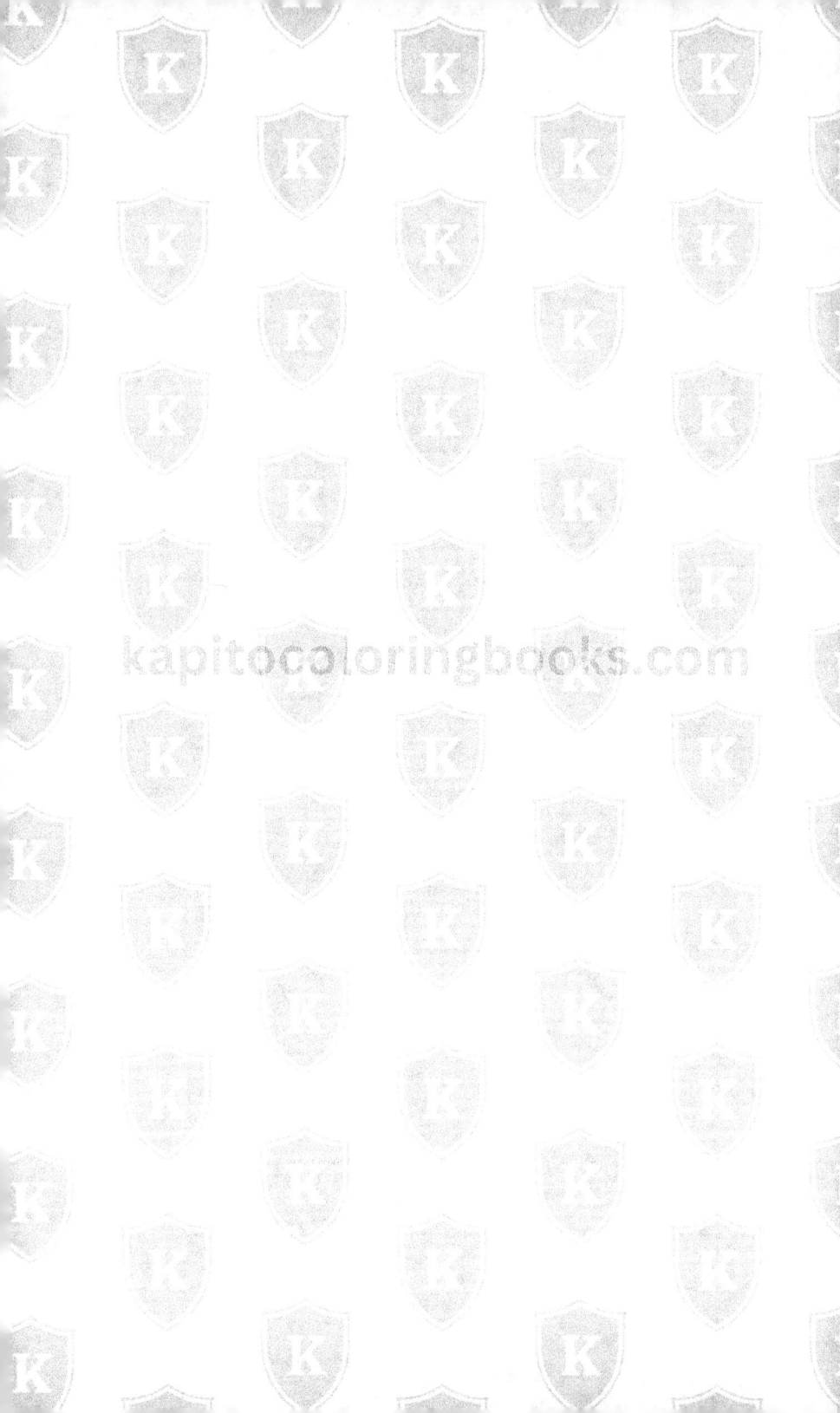